Advance Praise for Public Policy Argumentation and Debate

"*Public Policy Argumentation and Debate: A Practical Guide for Advocacy* offers a unique and timely solution to a frequent classroom problem: students' lack of preparation to credibly and substantively engage in public discourse. The book rigorously identifies what students of public argument must know. It is lucidly presented, and made even more accessible through its use of contemporary examples and case studies. As such, the book is profoundly successful in accomplishing its stated goal of helping to cultivate 'an instructional environment that encourages people to engage the controversies of their time and place.' It will become standard reading in all of my courses where public discourse and political advocacy are central concerns, and argument a necessary skill—which is to say, all of them."

—Charlton McIlwain, Associate Professor of Media, Culture, and Communication, New York University; Co-author of the award-winning book *Race Appeal* (2011)

"Philip Dalton and John R. Butler provide a well-structured, clear, and comprehensive guide to practical argumentation. Commensurate with their experience as both formal debaters and professors of argument and public advocacy, they balance rigorous argumentation concepts with the realistic needs of students and citizen advocates for whom a course might be their only formal advocacy training. Practical elements like the 'critical questions' that run throughout give the student immediately useable tools for building and understanding public argument. I especially like that the book sticks to a clear mission. Too often argumentation books seek to be histories of rhetoric, to theorize rhetoric, and to be practical guides for formal intercollegiate debate and public advocacy all at once. The result is often a diluted and much less useable textbook that confuses students. *Public Policy Argumentation and Debate* presents focused, cohesive, and very readable explanations. This book is ideal for use as a main text for general guidance in the practice of advocacy."

—David Worth, Director of Forensics, Rice University

"*Public Policy Argumentation and Debate* explores the theories and practical applications of argumentation and debate through examples and activities that meet students where they live. The text addresses a common learning outcome of undergraduate core curricula to develop critical thinking skills. Philip Dalton and John R. Butler provide the basic tools for students to unravel and participate in public policy arguments in a wide variety of settings."

—Diana Bartelli Carlin, Associate Vice President for Graduate Education & International Initiatives and Professor of Communication, Saint Louis University

Public Policy Argumentation and Debate

This book is part of the Peter Lang Media and Communication list.
Every volume is peer reviewed and meets
the highest quality standards for content and production.

PETER LANG
New York • Bern • Frankfurt • Berlin
Brussels • Vienna • Oxford • Warsaw

Philip Dalton | John R. Butler

Public Policy Argumentation and Debate

A Practical Guide for Advocacy

PETER LANG
New York • Bern • Frankfurt • Berlin
Brussels • Vienna • Oxford • Warsaw

Library of Congress Cataloging-in-Publication Data
Dalton, Philip.
Public policy argumentation and debate: a practical guide for advocacy /
Philip Dalton, John R. Butler.
pages cm
Includes bibliographical references and index.
1. Debates and debating. 2. Rhetoric. 3. Policy sciences.
4. Communication—Political aspects. I. Butler, John R. II. Title.
PN4181.D25   808.53—dc23   2014040315
ISBN 978-1-4331-1168-6 (hardcover)
ISBN 978-1-4331-1167-9 (paperback)
ISBN 978-1-4539-1470-0 (e-book)

Bibliographic information published by **Die Deutsche Nationalbibliothek**.
Die Deutsche Nationalbibliothek lists this publication in the "Deutsche
Nationalbibliografie"; detailed bibliographic data are available
on the Internet at http://dnb.d-nb.de/.

Cover design by Gregg Rojewski, using images from the auditorium
of Painters District Council No. 30 in Aurora, Illinois.

The paper in this book meets the guidelines for permanence and durability
of the Committee on Production Guidelines for Book Longevity
of the Council of Library Resources.

To...

M. Jack Parker, Dorothy Bishop, Martha Cooper, and Robert P. Newman
The teachers and coaches who taught us how to argue.

TABLE OF CONTENTS

ACKNOWLEDGMENTS

After we decided to write a book about public policy advocacy, our minds returned to when and how we initially encountered the various concepts that make up our understanding of argumentation and debate. Doing so reminded us of our experience as members of NIU Forensics and working with the people at Northern Illinois University who generously devoted their careers to teaching us, and countless others, how to argue. Every memory we have of these extraordinary mentors – M. Jack Parker, Dorothy Bishop, and Martha Cooper – is cherished. We were so fortunate to have had time with them in that exciting intellectual environment. While they are no longer with us, and therefore could not assist us in the development of this project, we hope the lessons and guidance we have assembled here is a clear indication of the significance of their influence on us and the discipline of rhetoric and communication. All three serve today as models for us as we chart our paths in the academy and professional communication environments. John had the added good fortune to work for a time with the legendary Robert P. Newman, who taught him and many others that advocacy is at its best when it is aimed in the direction of justice. This book is dedicated to these four teachers, coaches, scholars, and advocates.

We each are fortunate to share our lives with people whose generosity and encouragement were critical to the publication of this book. Phil is grateful to his wife Lisa Dalton for absorbing an unfair share of the child rearing duties for their boys – Eli and Parker – while he undertook the task of co-authoring this book. John wishes to acknowledge the patience and support of his mother Sharon Butler, sister Jane McCarthy, and partner Ricardo Gomez Renteria, who saw much less of him than usual because of this project and listened to his lengthy explanations and concepts while they were being developed. Both of us are grateful to our employers and colleagues for their support of our work. Phil wishes to recognize Hofstra University for the resources they provided, in terms of both the teaching releases and funding that were crucial to the completion of this project. John is thrilled to work with the leaders of the Painters District Council No. 30, with whom he has addressed a variety of exciting practical advocacy challenges. John also wishes to acknowledge lessons he has learned about advocacy as a member of the board of trustees at Northern Illinois University and to thank his board colleagues and the many talented students, faculty, staff, and administrators at NIU for their role in forming his perspectives and approaches to public policy advocacy.

Both of us wish to thank Mary Savigar, senior acquisitions editor at Peter Lang, and an insightful reviewer who offered much needed guidance, for devoting their time to this project. Finally, we wish to extend our highest regards to each other. Throughout this and other scholarly projects, we have developed mutual respect and admiration for each other as scholars, teachers, and advocates and the trust required to blend our voices in the hopes of making a difference.

Philip Dalton and John Butler, September 2014

PREFACE

The two of us entered the world of argumentation and debate at just about the same time, both as undergraduates at Northern Illinois University studying political science in the early 1990s. When we joined NIU's debate team, we came from similar backgrounds: both from working-class suburbs west and south of Chicago, both from families who valued education as a route to political and economic empowerment, and both interested and involved in political issues. It is fair to say also that we began higher education with a lot to learn. We were full of opinions, but, like many of our readers, we suspect, our elementary and secondary education experiences did not leave us with a comprehensive understanding of history, politics, and science upon which to draw conclusions with any certainty, or the research, writing, and analytical skills required to piece together alternatives to policy directions we did not support. We were very ambitious, full of outrage and discontent, and never short of opinions. Even religion, while present in our family systems to varying degrees, was not a major force in our conscious sensemaking, and offered us few certain answers. It is not surprising to us today that our search for a system through which we could filter what we learned, and enable us to determine how to use it, would lead us to the study of argumentation and debate.

While we did not know it at the time, joining the debate team at NIU was tantamount to being brought on board a particularly styled vessel, piloted by a captain and first officer. We would learn later that the coaching team of M. Jack Parker and Dorothy Bishop, both faculty members in NIU's Department of Communication, had invited many other students to become part of their teaching and learning community. Once we found ourselves safely inside the unfamiliar vessel, we marveled at its gears and levers and were quick to agree to stay on board.

When students are first introduced to the academic field of argumentation and debate, typically unbeknownst to them at the time, they find themselves in vessels that are designed to function in particular ways. Their "captains" – teachers, if they are in a classroom; coaches, if they are joining a debate team – often undergo a similar experience with their own captains and vessels. Only if they continue to study argumentation might they learn some of the mechanics behind the facades of gears and levers and some about the engineers who built them. These metaphorical vessels might be called intellectual traditions, ancestral lines of thinking and teaching that formed communities across generations that have passed on knowledge and skills in particular ways. In the study of argumentation, many of these communities have read the same foundational texts – Aristotle's *On Rhetoric*, Cicero's *De Inventione*, and other works to which the field of argument owes its origins – but each creates, presents, and engages in advocacy within unique frameworks and formats derived both from textbooks and less formally passed on through coaching protocols.

The intellectual tradition of our perspective can be found most vividly described in the 1963 work of Robert B. Huber, *Influencing through Argument*.[1] *Influencing through Argument* was the culmination of several years of learning and teaching argumentation by Huber, then a faculty member in the Department of Speech at the University of Vermont, and a community of colleagues and graduate students who worked with him, including the person who would become our debate coach, M. Jack Parker (the textbook was reissued in 2006 by Huber's student, Alfred Snider[2]). Huber formed an inventory of objections that incorporated many of the complex rules of logic, and formal and informal fallacies, that might take a student years to master. His self-titled "lines of argument" approach to explaining argumentation was an attempt, he explained, to "translate the tests of evidence, the tests of reasoning, and the methods by which fallacies can be revealed into language readily available to the student speaker."[3] Moreover, unlike the logicians of his time, Huber was aware he was helping students *both* analyze proposals *and* speak about them, noting that "the structuralizing of the types of reasoning available in a proposition of policy may help the student, not only in [his or her] analysis, but in the building of stronger speeches."[4] Huber's focus on a set of common objections in the teaching of argumentation and debate, and his particular interest in the role of argument in the making of public policy, offered us a framework for engaging the world of public policy, a world in which people use argument to influence others to alter the status quo – to alleviate what Huber called "evils"[5] – or maintain the status quo. Much has been written since, of course, by students of Huber and students of Huber's students, as well as by individuals whose intellectual traditions run along different lines. One exceptional work that we place within the legacy of Huber's approach is written by Martha Cooper. Cooper was once a graduate assistant working for Parker and Bishop and eventually joined them on the faculty at NIU. She became the master's degree advisor to this text's co-author, Phil Dalton, and for a brief time before her death, a departmental colleague of the other co-author, John Butler. In *Analyzing Public Discourse*, Cooper seeks to cull the practical tools from controversies playing out in the public sphere – where argumentation and debate was happening with real consequences for real people – from the increasingly technical study of argumentation geared toward the intercollegiate competitive debate community and its adherents – where argument was happening with no real consequences other than that some teams won and some teams lost. Consistent with Huber's lines of argument, her text places an emphasis on the "critical tools for analyzing messages."[6] Chapters titled "Good Reasons Fit the Audience," "Good Reasons Structure the Audience's Response," and "Good Reasons Withstand Objection" – the latter including subjects such as "Objections to Data," "Objections to Reasoning," and "Objections to Procedure," make clear her central interest in public policy advocacy as it is *practiced* by ordinary people.

The motivation behind Cooper's text is the same impulse that drove our argumentation and debate mentors to lifelong professional careers as teachers and debate coaches and the same impulse that drives us to write this book: a desire to teach people to marshal their capacity to argue. Rhetorical scholar and debate coach Gordon Mitchell has given this capacity the term "argumentative agency," a term that signifies the *impulse* to resist the status quo or challenges to the status quo and a willingness to act on that impulse.[7] Approaches to the teaching of argumentation and debate that seek to foster argumentative agency, particularly in the realm of public policy, meet the challenge put forth by Mitchell, who criticizes the laboratory approach to academic debate training:

> To the extent that the academic space begins to take on characteristics of a lab-oratory, the barriers demarcating such a space from other spheres of deliberation beyond the school grow taller and less permeable. When such barriers reach insur-mountable dimensions, argumentation in the academic setting unfolds on a purely simulated plane, with students practicing critical thinking and advocacy skills in strictly hypothetical thought-spaces. Although they may research and track public argument as it unfolds outside the confines of the laboratory for research purposes, in this approach, students witness argumentation beyond the walls of the academy as spectators, with little or no apparent recourse to directly participate or alter the course of events.[8]

Mitchell says a lot in the above quote, and we do not expect all of our readers to appreciate the cause to which he so eloquently commits himself; suffice it to say, we offer this book as one approach that attempts to bridge that gap between the concepts used in the "laboratory" of the classroom and the public controversies in which individuals are presently engaged and may someday become engaged.

The challenge is how to develop an *instructional* environment that en-courages people to engage the controversies of their time and place. Too often, in our opinion, argumentation and debate teachers limit their role to what Mitchell refers to as "preparatory pedagogy" in "hypothetical thought-spaces." Preparatory pedagogy, as the term suggests, focuses on *future* advocacy. It is also a practice steeped in assumptions and conventional wisdom about the sheer power and emancipatory potential of learning how to argue, such as the belief that students will be "hooked" the moment they experience an actual formal debate round and will continue from that point into a life character-ized by high levels of argumentative agency. Seldom have we found the allure of the debate round to be as formative. For every student who is captivated by academic debate, ten quietly never return for subsequent instruction. It is impossible to know with certainty why or what becomes of them, but we have a sinking suspicion they leave feeling like the world of public policy advocacy is not for them, that it is a world made up of culturally powerful, naturally intelligent, and articulate individuals. We suspect the disenfranchised have an idealistic notion of competency in advocacy, likely fueled by images in the news and entertainment media that predominantly feature white males in the exercise of social and political power in formal deliberative spaces, such as the floors of legislatures, or "experts" who have been invited to contribute their opinions due to a level of educational and career achievement that is difficult to imagine as a personal accomplishment.

Something must be done to convince more people that their opinions matter, that they can lead, or contribute productively to, an effort to change the status quo or defend it against changes that will produce disadvantages. You may be ready for a full court press or you may need to develop argumentative agency more incrementally. You may need to repair some of the damage done to you through parenting, schooling, and the media. If you are less argumentative, simply becoming aware of activity or behavior with which you disagree may be the first order of business. You should know it is ok to disagree and that doing so is essential to the development of good public policy. Then, perhaps, you can be motivated to learn how to express your disagreement.

We intend this book as a guide to facilitating and aligning your argumentative agency. We set out to provide a primer for translating the systems of academic debate for your use in the actual practice of public policy advocacy. While knowledge of argument theory can inform how you advocate in actual practice, the connections between theory and practice will not always be clear. The apparent role a proposition plays in an academic debate, for instance, is considerably different than its place in public policy advocacy. The capacity to recognize where your advocacy fits under a proposition provides important information you can use to guide your message development efforts.

In our effort to help you better understand the application of argument theory to public policy advocacy and develop your capacity to confidently engage advocacy situations, we unfold four general threads of instruction. We weave these threads throughout the chapters, and they should become noticeably more relevant to the practical negotiation of advocacy situations as we delve more deeply into the content.

First, each of our chapters centers on standard argumentation and debate textbook content; however, we attempt to broaden your understanding of this content in relation to public policy advocacy. We provide a variety of illustrations and examples that span a wide range of advocacy situations, including local settings and situations that may be familiar to you. As such, this text can profitably accompany and complement traditional argumentation and debate textbooks, or it can function as a basic guide for individuals and organizations involved in controversies or engaged in advocacy campaigns.

Second, in addition to encouraging you to enter the controversies that concern you, we seek to convince you that you can develop compelling advocacy. Message development is an evolving capacity, a skill that improves over time as you learn more about the world and expose yourself to opportunities to offer your opinion. Toward this objective, we focus on the role of reasoning and evidence as the building blocks of compelling advocacy. In public policy advocacy, you will develop messages through engagement with others and will be limited by situational constraints. To rely on a metaphor to illustrate this point, developing advocacy is much like making a meal for your family. You encounter family members demanding specific things and refusing to accept other options. The resulting meal is limited considerably by your available supplies and perhaps financial resources, and there are relationship issues with which you must contend, such as whose preferences should be given the most weight in the decision, how to divide the preparation responsibilities, and so forth. Your actual advocacy messages are often a product of your thoughtful use of available resources guided by a carefully nuanced effort to address the needs of your target audience within the constraints of a particular setting.

Third, we strive to impart a framework for public policy advocacy wherein you and your target audience belong, for all practical purposes, to the same community. On a practical level, this means that you can assume you possess the capacity to assess the particulars of an advocacy situation and craft appealing messages based on that assessment. Moreover, as you will learn in the chapters on reasoning and evidence, we believe commonalities that derive from being part of the same community also form a common rationality that you can rely on for the practical purpose of developing messages. This common rationality, while not always practically in operation, is an important creative assumption, because it permits you to expect advocacy to conform to general structural norms and to pose several universal questions when developing your advocacy – what we refer to as "critical questions." We appreciate that there are several situations when these assumptions may not lead you to the most effective appeals, and we understand that well-funded advocacy campaigns may benefit from more precise audience analysis protocols, both qualitative and quantitative. And, we appreciate the limits of such assumptions when your advocacy is directed to wider cultural, international, and global audiences. Nevertheless, we view these assumptions as critical to your adoption of a constructive framework when you are presented with the practical need to develop compelling messages in response to an actual controversy. As noted at the end of this Preface, our objective is to give you a starting point, a foundation on which you may build an ever-improving capacity to engage the important issues in your worlds.

Fourth, we encourage you to focus on the contextual nature of public policy advocacy – that your advocacy is situated in varied and complex settings that give rise to the events that cause you to engage in advocacy. The particularities of these settings inform what you say, when and where your advocacy begins, the degree of emphasis you place on certain arguments, and any particular efforts to reach a cross-section of an audience. Your awareness of this context is not the same, in our view, as an appreciation for the needs of an audience. Drawing from rhetorical theory, we view contextual considerations as an awareness of norms that have significant implications on the construction of your advocacy and the manner in which it is received.

In chapter one, we provide an orientation to argument that reconciles some general argument theory with our practical approach to advocacy. We consider public policy advocacy necessary for solving problems, particularly in a society that values political participation. Today's democratic institutions necessitate broad participation in the process of identifying problems and giving reasoned consideration to proposed solutions. Wading into such a system can appear daunting and futile for many. Nevertheless, the only way to ensure that policy will reflect your preferences or objections is to give voice to your ideas. Skillful advocates voice their opinions in ways that help them attain audience consideration, which means their advocacy is supported with reliable evidence, well-reasoned, sustained, clear, adapted to audiences and the setting, and both ethical and persuasive.

In chapter two, we focus on the role of propositions in public policy advocacy. For the student of argumentation and debate, the proposition is an affirmatively worded sentence calling for some action (X should do Y), which provides an occasion to debate. In public advocacy situations, however, propositions are rarely stated. Identifying the proposition enables you to better understand the role and probable impact of your advocacy. We urge you to determine the proposition under which your advocacy is situated as a first step in identifying the burdens you have within an advocacy situation.

In chapter three, we introduce you to what are commonly referred to as "stock issues" in academic debate. Students of argumentation and debate are instructed to use the stock issues of policy argument to ensure that their arguments are complete (that, indeed, they have met their argumentative burdens). In public policy advocacy, stock issues often define the boundaries of a controversy for advocates: *what are the sides arguing about?* Stock issues, in this regard, constitute the "anatomy of public policy argument" – (a) what is the problem, (b) what causes the problem, (c) what solution is being proposed, and (d) will that solution likely solve the problem? Answers to these questions can provide all advocates operating within a controversy a better understanding of their obligations during an episode of argument within the larger framework of an advocacy campaign.

In chapters four and five, we explore the role of reasoning in public policy advocacy. While we offer a theoretical summary of the common forms of reasoning, our primary focus is on understanding how reasoning is used and on what we term "critical questions" used by advocates and target audiences to determine an argument's infrastructure. A student trained in the types of reasoning may attempt to look for the explicit appearance of particular methods of reasoning in actual argument, but how advocates reason is rarely made clear or explicit. That is to say, reasoning is often implied; thus a focus of chapter four is the value and process of identifying the relative contribution of a reasoning structure that may need to be uncovered before it can be effectively addressed. Following this point, we focus on the most common form of reasoning in public policy advocacy: causal reasoning – where we situate many of the standard objections occasioned by public policy advocacy. In chapter five, we examine several additional forms of reasoning that undergird arguments presented within public policy controversies. Throughout, critical questions are provided for each form of reasoning. These critical questions function as tools for constructing and responding to advocacy.

In chapters six and seven, we explore the role and use of evidence in public policy advocacy. In chapter six, we provide a theoretical perspective for considering the role of evidence within the infrastructure of an argumentative appeal. Audiences often presume the existence of sound evidence where none at all has been presented. Other times, audiences fail to subject evidence to appropriate scrutiny. We revisit some of the formative lessons about evidence, relying heavily on the framework provided by Robert P. Newman and Dale R. Newman in their seminal text, *Evidence*.[9] In our view, not only do Newman and Newman provide an essential means of considering evidence in public policy advocacy; they do so in a manner that, when applied to contemporary policy issues, offers accessible theoretical tenets essential for your policymaking activities. Moreover, in considering the role of ideology, Newman and Newman, and later works of Robert Newman (whom co-author John Butler studied under at the University of Pittsburgh), form a useful framework for uncovering the ideological underpinnings that inform the creation, selection, and use of particular evidence. With this theoretical framework for considering evidence laid out, we provide – in chapter seven – critical questions you can use as tools for evaluating evidence. Specifically, we consider evidence derived from authorities and statistics and provide critical questions as efficient ways for evaluating such types of evidence.

In chapter eight, we focus on the audience of public advocacy and how careful consideration of a targeted audience can help strengthen your advocacy efforts. Our conception of the target audience is grounded in a particular view of the audience as a community to which advocates belong. As part of your own community, the target audience is an entity you engage in a shared pursuit of good policy.

Finally, in chapter nine, we consider the dynamics of the advocacy setting. In addition to audience, your willingness and ability to adapt to the setting also influences the quality of your advocacy. Assuming that most advocacy events will require you to make your case orally or in writing, we emphasize the importance of accommodating the norms of an advocacy setting. Different occasions or events give rise to advocacy, and a one-size-fits-all approach will have limited success. Specific circumstances that give an advocacy event its character may also be considered, such as exigency, history, speaker-audience relationship, relevant cultural concerns, audience psychology, and physical space. Finally, we consider mediated advocacy, contrasting in-person advocacy with advocacy that is mediated. We recommend being mindful of the capacity of various forms of media to enhance distribution and reception of advocacy, but we warn against the ways different media can compromise the control you have over your messages.

Within each chapter, we also provide a list of "takeaways" and an exercise designed to guide your personal engagement with public policy advocacy. We state the takeaways briefly, and they are more along the lines of learning objectives and main points than summaries of chapter content. Our intention in providing exercises is to have you identify where and how concepts found in each chapter might manifest in everyday advocacy. By having you survey and analyze public discussions of policy in real time, it is our hope that you will develop a greater command of these issues and an improved understanding of the role of argumentation and debate in the public policy context.

If you have significant experience in the worlds of academic and intercollegiate competitive debate, you may find throughout this book that we make several statements with a degree of confidence and certainty that may not ring true with the way you were introduced to policy debate. We do not contend that the system we assembled for this textbook will apply perfectly to all public advocacy situations, and certainly we do not expect our framework to match conventional means of preparing students for academic debate contests. Our goal is to inspire your thoughtful and ethical entry into the public policy world, where many new lessons will be learned. The sooner you reach beyond the ideas in this book to develop more complex world views and a sense of civic responsibility, as far as we are concerned, the better.

Notes

1. Robert B. Huber, *Influencing through Argument* (New York: David McKay Company, 1963).
2. Robert B. Huber and Alfred C. Snider, *Influencing through Argument* (Updated Edition) (New York: International Debate Education Association, 2006).
3. Huber, v.
4. Ibid., v.
5. Ibid., 236.
6. Martha Cooper, *Analyzing Public Discourse* (Long Grove, IL: Waveland Press, 1989), x.
7. Gordon Mitchell, "Pedagogical Possibilities for Argumentative Agency in Academic Debate," *Argumentation and Advocacy* 35, 2 (1998).
8. Ibid., 43.
9. Robert P. Newman and Dale R. Newman, *Evidence* (Boston, MA: Houghton Mifflin Company, 1969).

· 1 ·

AN ORIENTATION TO PUBLIC POLICY ADVOCACY

Takeaways

1. Argument is essential for the proper function of a democratic governing system. That system relies on you to voice your opinions and to subject others' ideas to careful scrutiny.
2. Public policy advocacy is a positive and constructive activity that will engage you in public conversations about the merits of policy proposals.

Introduction

No one has ever learned how to ride a bike by reading about it. All skills, to some extent, must be practiced to be mastered, and there is no use in mastering a skill unless you intend to use it. Though you have been arguing throughout your life, formal theories about argumentation and debate broaden the knowledge you already have, enabling you to become a better advocate before different audiences and within different settings. In short, learning to argue skillfully requires knowledge *and* practice. We wrote this book suspecting you have already developed an understanding of argument. Perhaps you learned about argument in an academic setting, or you may have developed your knowledge through trial and error in some professional capacity. By formally studying argumentation and debate, you indicate your desire to enhance your skills and expand your repertoire. In this text, we instruct you to apply several formal concepts to "real-world" public policy advocacy situations.

At the core of public policy controversies are issues. An issue is a matter of public concern about which parties disagree. Disputing parties typically disagree about (a) whether there is a problem that warrants a solution, (b) what causes the problem, (c) whether a proposed solution will alleviate the problem, and/or (d) whether the advantages of a proposal are greater than the disadvantages. A defining characteristic of public policymaking is that the outcomes of decisions cannot be determined until after we execute plans. *Will this tax cut help the economy? Is this war winnable? Will this new form of public transportation reduce carbon emissions?* Humans can be very intelligent, but they cannot precisely predict the future. About the above questions, advocates can only make predictions that are supported by evidence and are well-reasoned, and they base their decisions on those predictions.

Democracy assumes that disputing parties will disagree about issues in a shared pursuit of good policy, which is a policy that solves a problem without causing other new problems that are more troubling than the original problem. For residents of democratic societies, the pursuit of good policy occurs within a governmental system within which people have the capacity to shape the character of their communities by enlisting the support of others for their ideas. The champions of democracy wrested authority from outmoded governing systems, replacing them with democratic systems that assume residents will develop good policy by relying on valid evidence and sound reasoning. As a result, the legitimacy of policies relies not only on gaining support within a democratic system but also on the level of public participation leading up to the adoption of policies.

In this chapter, we make a general case for why argument is good, countering some of the attitudes people have about argument that prevent them from participating in public policy advocacy. Next, we make the case for full and thoughtful public participation. Finally, we describe a conception of good public policy advocacy.

Argument's "Bad Rap"

Those who devote a significant amount of their lives studying and teaching others how to argue are constantly encountering the bad rap that argument, as an activity and term, has within certain circles of society. We have each experienced multiple occasions when we have used the term "argue" in settings where argument is common, only to be corrected by someone who responds with, "I don't think 'argue' is the right word," or something to that effect. Preferring terms such as "discussion" or "advise," implicit in their admonishment and alternative terminology is a popular association of argument with negative speech acts like verbal aggression and combativeness. There is little surprise considering popular depictions of disagreement often involve yelling, screaming, swearing, threats, and belittling. *The Jersey Shore*, *Kitchen Nightmares*, *The O'Reilly Factor*, *Nancy Grace*, and *The Jerry Springer Show* are a few examples of shows depicting people dealing with disagreement in aggressive ways. Tapping into a commonly held attitude toward argument, shows like *The Daily Show* and *The Colbert Report* lampoon American public deliberative processes and systems. Even when the subject of debate is treated with seriousness and respect, argument's bad rap is present. In the September 2012 special issue of *The Atlantic*, carrying James Fallows serial article on who will win the presidential debates, the cover and interior images show a fictional boxing match between challenger Mitt Romney and incumbent Barack Obama, and the article is titled "Slugfest." The downside of this popular framing is reinforcement of a cynical notion that there is something anti-social and uncivilized about argument, and participation in a debate is as futile as participation in a physical fight.

In addition to the popular depictions of arguments that negatively shape our perceptions of the activity, you may also fear that, regardless of the reasonableness of your claims or concerns, challenging others will damage your relationship with them. This phenomenon has been described as a conflict between *instrumental* aspects of a message versus *expressive* aspects of a message.[1] If you could somehow remove all relational dynamics from a communication situation, the words you use to communicate information and persuasive messages about a topic (instrumental aspects of a message) might be received as perfectly respectful and reasonable communication. Those same words, however, like it or not, also reflect and shape the relationship between you and the persons with whom you are communicating (expressive aspects of a message). Due to this expressive quality of communication, an unintended consequence of your advocacy may be that the people you are communicating with interpret your words as both a rejection of their ideas and a negative assessment of their intellect and other aspects of their personhood. Because of the anticipation of argument's expressive qualities, people often avoid engaging in argument. After all, it is only natural to want people to like and agree with you.

Another reason some may have adopted a negative disposition toward argument is that they perceive argumentation to be a highly technical and mysterious skill, requiring a mastery of technique. Many competitive college debaters experience moments when friends refuse to argue with them for fear that their debating skills will give them an unfair advantage, as though debate experience can make an argument appear better than it is. And sometimes, skilled arguers *do* bully opponents with forceful language and displays of nonverbal confidence, which, of course, does nothing to advance the pursuit of good policy.

Ironically then, negative perceptions of argument may cause you to believe that something constructive can be achieved by avoiding it. You may believe the harmony of the community will be better served by avoiding a prolonged debate. People often express a desire to see less conflict over public policy; many claim to want "bipartisanship" and "compromise," conceiving these terms as somehow precluding argumentation. The goal of compromise can be troubling, if viewed this way, because in matters of public policy the stakes can be enormous; inadequate criticism of policy ideas can have destructive consequences.

An important by-product of argumentation and debate training is the awareness that the constructive outcomes of argument, particularly when done well, outweigh the expressive elements of argument that turn people off. After all, your decision *not to argue* is a policy decision; disengagement is an indirect, and often unintended, endorsement of the status quo. Also, debate introduces you to different ways of seeing the world. Such openness can expose you to superior policy alternatives and criticisms that may not have occurred to you. A satisfying engagement with the subject of argument, whether through formal instruction or actual practice, will help thaw your resistance to argument in ways that cause you to perceive it for the positive and constructive activity that it can be and often is and thus prepare you to participate in public policymaking.

Public Policy Advocacy and the Political System

That a society is a democracy (a federal democracy in the case of the United States) means much more than that people vote for individuals to represent them in legislative and administrative offices. The central reason that democratic practice emerged out of the monarchies of Western Europe is because the assumption that reasonable people could evaluate ideas and make decisions *as well, if not better*, than monarchs, gained credence among the property-owning class. In 1644, John Milton, in his *Areopagitica*, asserted that truth prevails in a "free and open encounter."[2] John Stuart Mill wrote in 1859, in *On Liberty*, that, "Wrong opinions and practices gradually yield to fact and argument: but facts and arguments, to produce any effect on the mind, must be brought before it."[3] This attitude is evident in the Supreme Court's free speech ruling in the 1919, *Abrams vs. United States*. In that ruling, Justice Oliver Wendell Holmes writes:

> ... the best test of truth is the power of the thought to get itself accepted in the competition of the market, and that truth is the only ground upon which their wishes safely can be carried out. That at any rate is the theory of our Constitution.[4]

The "marketplace of ideas" is a metaphor that finds its origins in Adam Smith's writings about capitalism's ability to reward the best products through mass consumer consumption. By applying this notion to ideas, or public policy, many scholars and thinkers, and generations of students of argumentation, have accepted the idea that policy proposals that survive or prevail in a debate are the "best" proposals. While surviving public scrutiny may not necessarily ensure that a policy is good, public debate is still, according to many, the best mechanism for vetting public policy proposals.

The alternative to public scrutiny is silence, and its consequences are almost always less desirable than public argument. "The squeaky wheel gets the grease" is a commonly used idiom that captures an important political reality: opinions must be voiced and advocated in order to be given public consideration. The lack of an opinion's expression may guarantee that the public ignores it. Elisabeth Noelle-Neumann warns of the public communication phenomenon she terms the "spiral of silence" – when silence begets silence because the impression that one's opinion is a minority position discourages the minority from voicing it.[5] This process, she explains, continues (spirals downward) until the position is rarely heard at all. And when it *is* expressed at a much later point in time, its novelty renders it more readily dismissed by the public as a fringe argument.

What Is Public Policy Advocacy?

You have engaged in virtually every species of argument at some point in your life, thus explaining what argument *is* ought to involve less a definition of it than an explanation of what comprises it. Martha Cooper defined argument for the ordinary person as "reasons," writing, "when advocates present arguments, they present reasons that justify their positions."[6] Public policy advocacy, in this regard, is comprised of reasons that support proposals in opposition to, or defense of, the status quo. Different argument types place different burdens on advocates. This book is about one particular type of argument often referred to, in its most basic sense, as "deliberative" argument. Deliberative argument deals with matters of the future – *What should be done?* This differs from two other types of argument commonly referred to as "forensic" and "epideictic" argument. Forensic argument is about matters of the past. It is commonly thought of as legal argument, such as that practiced in a courtroom. Similar to fictional forensic scientists on television, who attempt to establish how someone died by weaving pieces of evidence into a likely scenario, a forensic *argument* may focus on whether something did or did not happen or whether someone did or did not do something. Epideictic argument, on the other hand, deals with matters of the present, and that typically means argument that either praises or blames something or someone. Public university administrators blaming their state legislature for failing to properly support higher education is epideictic argument. Epideictic argument also often functions to reinforce social values held by people in the present. A eulogy at a memorial, for example, will employ epideictic argument to extol the admirable qualities of the deceased and call on the audience to adopt these same qualities.

Policy argument's focus on future action gives it its defining characteristic: that it is concerned with predictions. *Will natural gas fracking in New York's upstate watershed pollute the state's freshwater supply? Will income tax increases slow or reduce job creation?* Because we cannot know the future, on matters of public policy we are left to deal in predictions, which are matters of probability. Thus, when you engage in public policy advocacy, you assert *probable* future outcomes of a proposed policy. To do this effectively, public policy advocacy relies on evidence and reasoning to determine the best courses of action.

According to rhetorical scholar Thomas Goodnight, the capacity of this type of "public argument" to yield "a probable answer to questions of preferable conduct" is a desirable "alternative to decisions based on authority or blind chance."[7]

Goodnight provides further insight as to what comprises public policy advocacy. One central facet of argument in the "public sphere" is that its consequences extend beyond the "personal" and "technical" spheres – other settings in which argument occurs. Argument in the public sphere is also situated between the formal standards for evidence and reasoning of technical settings and the informal demands of private settings. In other words, what is accepted as legitimate argument in the astrophysicist's lab differs remarkably from what is accepted at the Thanksgiving table; how someone argues in a public forum lies somewhere in between. Students of argument may find it useful to delve more deeply into knowledge about argumentation in order to accommodate the knowledge, attitudes, and capacities of the audience they plan to address.

The skillful adaptation of public arguments to audiences involves adapting evidence and reasoning to the people to whom you are speaking. As an advocate, when developing advocacy, you must consider more than merely what *you* find persuasive; what is persuasive to you may be thoroughly unconvincing to your audience. This is made more complex when you acknowledge the many facets of an audience. Identifying a target audience or audiences and choosing the proper places to start your advocacy require knowledge, thought, skill, and resources. Further complicating the notion of "audience" is the idea that the audience may be constituted (called into existence) *by* argument. Your advocacy can make individuals aware of an issue and activate their concern about it. A person in Redwood City, California, may have no knowledge of the existence of like-minded individuals in Fort Wayne, Indiana, or Valdosta, Georgia, but public policy advocacy can bring such people together and transform them into a defined target audience. Public policy advocates generate awareness of shared needs among people, and such people may form a "public" – a phenomenon that is a testament to the power of argument to generate a shared concern. Accomplishing this takes knowledge and skill beyond that which you have informally honed in your everyday experiences. Audiences are constituted by collections of "demographic" and "psychographic" groups or issue-aligned communities that coalesce because of, and around, public policy advocacy. Rhetorical scholar Michael Calvin McGee maintains that knowledge and understanding of issues *produce* a "people" or public. He describes "the people" as "a fiction dreamed by an advocate and infused with an artificial, rhetorical reality by the agreement of an audience to participate in a collective fantasy."[8] There may be no material ties between people who are connected by the shared abstract interests brought to their attention by advocacy, but they nevertheless exist as an entity that can be addressed.

What Is Good Public Policy Advocacy?

Now that we have described some of what comprises public policy advocacy, a natural next step is to offer guidance on what makes public policy advocacy "good." This is, after all, what you are striving for, why you are reading this book, and the goal behind all serious policymaking endeavors. Good public policy advocacy is not measured by persuasiveness alone. We maintain that the factual veracity, soundness, and contributions to civic participation, community, and public policymaking produced by such advocacy make it essential to our political system. After all, little good may come from a persuasive but poorly developed and under-scrutinized policy proposal. To the contrary, an under-scrutinized policy may generate tremendous harm.

Good public policy advocacy involves arguments that are *made*

Argument is by its nature good. Countless people refuse to participate in public controversies, failing to share their personal experiences, knowledge, reasoning, and preferences. These individuals are perhaps concerned they are bad arguers, they will not be listened to, or their argumentation will disrupt the harmony of the community. Regardless of the reason, their silence may cause like-minded people to conclude that their opinions are less valid, leading to a forfeiture of opportunities for community building and the development of social cooperation. Silence can also create power vacuums left open for other special interests to fill and contribute to perceptions of governing authorities as unresponsive to the needs of the people, particularly under-represented and marginalized communities. From our standpoint, arguments must be made as a first condition of good public policy advocacy.

Good public policy advocacy is *sustained*

Many advocates are frustrated when a target audience refuses to change its mind, even when confronted with what the advocates are convinced are airtight evidence and reasoning. Often it is an accomplishment, achieved over an extended period of time by a sustained advocacy effort, for an audience to agree that a problem even exists. It is far more helpful to think of such public advocacy instances as part of a larger *social controversy*. Kathryn Olson and Thomas Goodnight describe a social controversy's tendency to be "an *extended* rhetorical engagement" [emphasis added] as one of its defining characteristics.[9] We agree that good public policy advocacy often requires a commitment to a long view.

Good public policy advocacy has an *endpoint*

A proposed policy solution is the endpoint of public policy advocacy, the destination at which the advocate hopes to arrive. This means that to even begin to support or oppose an argument, it is wise to identify the objective of your advocacy – a policy – which may also be a central point or issue around which the controversy revolves. Once identified, if skillfully argued, this endpoint will have implications for every element of your argument; as an advocate, you seek to "take" your audience from its current position to a new "destination" by way of your skillful selection, arrangement, and delivery of evidence and reasoning.

Good public policy advocacy *withstands objections*

If public policy advocacy is supported by valid evidence and sound reasoning, it will withstand counter-argumentation or objections. This does not mean that good public appeals necessarily "win," though they may. If winning becomes your sole priority, you could merely employ modern public relations and marketing techniques to promote an idea. Its popularity, however, will not mean the idea has withstood scrutiny. In fact, drawing this conclusion is an *ad populum* fallacy – the false notion that because a majority agrees with something, it must be true. Instead of gauging an argument's quality on its popularity, its quality is more wisely gauged by its ability to withstand objections.

Good public policy advocacy is *crafted with an audience in mind*

The audience you target with your advocacy may already exist, or it may need to be called into existence. When the audience you have chosen to target already exists, you will likely consider the knowledge and attitudes of that audience when determining the starting points for that message. An existing audience is a group of people for whom the subject of your advocacy is already a matter of awareness or concern. There are advocacy situations in which the target audience will not exist, at least not as a group with a shared awareness and concern about your issue. This is often the case when there is little public awareness about the phenomenon you are addressing. When the audience does not exist, your advocacy must generate awareness and create a group of concerned people.

Good public policy advocacy *adapts to the setting*

The same argument delivered in two different settings will likely receive different reactions. You would not advocate for protection from mining pollutants in front of the U.S. Congress the same way you would at an outdoor labor rally; the forums are different. This is not merely a matter of different audiences; the setting itself may control the meaning of a message. The advocacy setting involves cultural norms and/or assumptions that shape expectations the audience may have related to an issue, or place constraints on advocates that can limit the range of available claims, structure language choices, and explain failures to communicate effectively. Good public policy advocacy considers the advocacy setting, including the medium through which the message is conveyed.

Good public policy advocacy is *ethical*

If the purpose of public argument is to select good policy, losing an argument can be a productive outcome. If your argument cannot withstand objection, there just might be a very good reason for that. Public policy advocacy is a problem-solving enterprise, and successful public scrutiny of ideas helps prevent the adoption of bad policy. If, however, you look at public policymaking strictly through a competitive lens, success is then measured only in terms of wins and losses. When winning becomes paramount, advocates risk becoming unethical by compromising honesty, failing to respect the audience, refusing to listen to opponents' valid claims, and losing track of the pursuit of the greatest advantages for the public.

Good public policy advocacy is *persuasive*

Persuasiveness is a component of good public advocacy because good ideas need champions. Writing about rhetoric, or the artful use of the means of persuasion, Aristotle explained in *On Rhetoric* that "things that are true and things that are just have a natural tendency to prevail over their opposites, so that if the decisions of judges are not what they ought to be, the defeat must be due to the speakers themselves, and they must be blamed accordingly."[10] The appropriate way for a message to come out, Aristotle explains, is in a way that makes it as persuasive as possible. You want to avoid having your message dull the persuasive force of your idea, evidence, and the reasoning used to support it. A stack of facts is not, by itself, persuasive. Instead, the message into which your facts are woven render them meaningful and moving to your listeners. Persuasive public policy advocacy requires the skillful application of the concepts of argumentation and rhetoric, including those outlined throughout this book.

In the next chapter, we discuss propositions, statements that assert that some agent of change should engage in some action, which serve as the point at which public policy advocacy begins.

Exercise 1: Considering Public Controversies as Arguments

Access the Internet and go to a major news media webpage. Consider the issues of the day and identify an issue that you care about personally. First, give the issue a creative name (e.g., "The trouble with Obamacare," "The warming earth," "Children on the border"). Second, describe the problem as you understand it. For the people concerned, what's going wrong and why is it bad? Or, what existing program, policy, activity, behavior, and so forth, is being questioned or criticized, and what are the consequences that, according to some, will follow efforts to change the way society addresses that program, policy, activity, behavior, and so forth? Third, assume the issue has at least two sides, and one is calling for a change, and the other is arguing that things should not be changed. What change is the first side calling for? Finally, identify some of the key players in the controversy. Give each side a creative name ("Proponents of [insert the change sought]" and "Opponents of [insert the change sought]") and describe some qualities of each (nations, political parties, community groups, labor unions, people who purchased a particular product, people who do not have health insurance, etc.).

Notes

1. Talcott Parsons, *The Social System* (Glencoe, IL: Free Press, 1951).
2. John Milton, *Milton's Areopagatica* (London: Spottiswoode & Co., 1873), 65.
3. John Stuart Mill, *On Liberty* (Boston, MA: Ticknor & Fields, 1863), 41.
4. Abrams vs. United States, 250 U.S. 616 (1919).
5. Elisabeth Noelle-Neumann, *The Spiral of Silence: Public Opinion – Our Social Skin* (Chicago: University of Chicago Press, 1993).
6. Martha Cooper, *Analyzing Public Discourse* (Long Grove, IL: Waveland Press, 1989), 50.
7. G. Thomas Goodnight, "The Personal, Technical, and Public Spheres of Argument: A Speculative Inquiry into the Art of Public Deliberation," *Journal of the American Forensic Association* 15 (1982), 214.
8. Michael Calvin McGee, "In Search of the People: A Rhetorical Alternative," *Quarterly Journal of Speech*, 61 (1975), 343.
9. Kathryn Olson and G. Thomas Goodnight, "Entanglements of Consumption, Cruelty, Privacy, and Fashion: The Social Controversy Over Fur," *Quarterly Journal of Speech*, 80 (1994), 249.
10. Aristotle, *On Rhetoric: A Theory on Civic Discourse*, trans. George Kennedy (Oxford: Oxford University Press, 2006), 6.

· 2 ·

PROPOSITIONS

Takeaways

1. Profitable public policy advocacy centers around endpoints that can be articulated in clear propositions.
2. Propositions define the boundaries of a controversy, helping you delineate what is, and what is not, germane to a public policy controversy.
3. Determining the proposition of an ongoing public policy controversy can help you understand the relationship and value of your own advocacy to the controversy.

Introduction

Whether you are effective when you advocate depends largely on whether you know precisely *for what* you are advocating. Propositions in the realm of public policy are statements that assert that some agent of change should engage in some action. That action is usually described in general terms with the understanding that a specific policy or plan will be advocated by proponents of change. Determining what the proposition is in a public controversy allows you to be purposeful and effective in your criticism of others' arguments and in your own advocacy. In chapter one, we explained that many arguments exist within prolonged social controversies involving multiple advocates representing different sides of issues, addressing different audiences, and operating in different advocacy settings. When you choose to enter a controversy, you may only be engaging a minor point among many; however there is almost always a larger argument to which minor points relate. By arguing your point, you may, intentionally or not, be participating in a larger debate – essentially a dispute over a proposition.

This chapter focuses on propositions because understanding what they are and how to identify them is the starting point for developing effective public policy advocacy. Because it is rare for a public policy controversy to be fully aired in one event or a single message, your ability to identify the proposition offers an opportunity to contemplate the contours of an ongoing controversy. By doing so, you become equipped to evaluate *which side you are on* and the strength of arguments offered by you and others. In this regard, the ability to identify a proposition in a public policy dispute becomes a practical skill that affects advocacy in multiple ways. We assist you in developing that skill by (a) considering the characteristics of ideal propositions, (b) examining some propositions in the context of actual controversies, and (3) distinguishing the different types of propositions – fact, value, and policy – with a particular focus on policy propositions.

Propositions: An Advocate's Thesis

A proposition is to an argument what a thesis is to an essay. It is a statement of the issue that is, in fact, the controversy. Robert Huber and Alfred C. Snider define the proposition as, "an assertion which an advocate intends to prove in the form of a complete sentence."[1] In actual practice, advocates rarely identify the larger issue that gives rise to their advocacy. This lack of propositional clarity is particularly evident in public controversies that consist of numerous episodes of argument. An American politician on CNN stating that cuts in the Greek government's spending on social programs has hurt the Greek economy might, for example, relate to a larger proposition concerning proposed government spending cuts in the United States. Though the proposition is unstated, an alert observer might conclude that Greek government spending would likely be discussed by an American politician because there was some American policy under consideration. The ability to relate this episode of argument to the unstated proposition under which it belongs would be very useful.

The distinction between a proposition and a "topic" is an important one. A topic is the subject of a message, while a proposition is an assertion advocates seek to prove. Consider U.S. involvement in Afghanistan. The topic may be "war," "taxes," or "debt spending," but the advocate's proposition is more likely something more specific ("The United States should train Afghanistan's military to be self-reliant," for example). Or, imagine yourself reading a blog post that you relate to the topic of global warming. You might conclude a blogger is arguing about global warming, but what about global warming is argued in the blog? *Is the planet warming? Is global warming part of a natural cycle? Is global warming caused by humans? Is global warming bad? Can global warming be prevented? Are the benefits of preventing or reversing global warming outweighed by the costs?* Instead of identifying the topic, after some analysis you might determine that the blog's author is claiming that, "The U.S. federal government should significantly limit the production of greenhouse gases." This proposition is a clear expression that allows you to determine where your beliefs lie in relation to it and what evidence and reasoning issues may arise as this proposition is debated. Without determining the proposition, advocates risk failing to fully identify and evaluate their argumentative burdens and points they may wish to express.

When forming a proposition or seeking to identify a proposition in an ongoing controversy, it is important to consider several common characteristics of propositions. Familiarity with these characteristics will help you better understand the central controversy, the divisions between sides in the controversy, and the issues and burdens for the respective sides. These characteristics are prescriptive, meaning they are *ideal*.

1. A proposition is a complete sentence

Ideally, propositions encapsulate whole thoughts within complete sentences. Distilling a public controversy down to a single sentence can be challenging, often because your personal points of engagement may only cover a small portion of the controversy. The act of formulating a proposition allows you to determine if, in fact, there is a single matter under dispute. When you cannot craft a single sentence, it is often a sign that your thinking is not yet clear on the matter or that you are blending arguments about two or more related topics that do not fall within the parameters of a single proposition. The central issues of a controversy and an indication of the endpoint of advocacy are captured in this single sentence. The sentence will typically include an agent of change as subject, followed by the verb "should," followed by some general description of a policy direction that differs from the status quo ("The Chicago City Council should seek the assistance of the Illinois National Guard to protect residents from neighborhood violence," for example).

2. A proposition is about one issue

While there may be many reasons for public policy disagreements, opposing sides typically disagree about a single larger matter. "The United States should provide military assistance to the Syria National Coalition" is a proposition about one issue. Advocates for the proposition may have plenty of reasons for calling for such an action and several specific policy scenarios; opponents, on the other hand, may oppose every possible action that reasonably fits under the call for action. Yet, when each of these clashes is considered, they amount to either support *for* or *against* the proposed action. For the purposes of public policy advocacy, the knowledge that a proposition focuses on one issue is most helpful when determining the single larger matter being disputed in a controversy. If you assume there is one issue being disputed, then you know to look for it. And, if or when you find multiple loci of disagreement, you can make the determination that either two separate propositions are under consideration, or all sides are, in fact, lining up under the same controversy.

Consider the following proposition: "The U.S. federal government should adopt policies that reduce the use of carbon fuels and encourage innovation in green energy solutions." Instead of one thought, this proposition includes *two* disputable points, and, as such, is poorly conceived. You can *agree* that carbon fuels should be reduced but *disagree* that green energy solutions should be encouraged. Because you disagree with one point, you technically disagree with the proposition, but do you? Maybe you support green energy but believe it should be "mandated" and not "encouraged." Such an attitude would put you squarely in support of a proposition advocating reductions in carbon emissions – the very matter, it appears, the original proposition attempted to articulate.

3. A proposition is a proposal to change the status quo

For the sake of clarity and developing the ability to effectively engage in public policy advocacy, we believe it is useful for you to assume that *all public policy propositions should call for a change in the status quo*. This assumption provides for clear and reliable division of responsibilities for which advocates can prepare and makes identifying the proposition for the purposes of such preparation much easier. To understand better, think of the status quo in the context of a forensic environment, in this example a courtroom. Just as the accused person in court is presumed innocent until proven guilty, the status quo too is considered sufficient until a compelling argument can be made to change it. Similar to a courtroom's prosecutor, a change advocate must explain what is *wrong* with the status quo. The change advocate has the burden to show that the status quo is insufficient and warrants change. This is often referred to as the "burden of proof" or "burden of evidence." For example, Americans presently live in an economy that relies heavily on energy derived from fossil fuels. Thus, the economic system presumes that fossil fuel consumption is acceptable. Those who would like to enact laws reducing carbon emissions resulting from fossil fuels are proposing a change to the status quo and have the burden of proving that the status quo causes a significant problem, one worth solving. Using the fossil fuel example, a good proposition might be, "The U.S. federal government should enact laws that mandate the reduction of fossil fuel use in America." This proposition clearly calls for a change in the status quo. A proposition that fails to call for a change in the status quo – "The U.S. federal government *should adopt no additional laws* that mandate the reduction of fossil fuel use in America," for example – makes little sense as an initiation point for advocacy, because advocates supporting such a proposition have no reason to call for or support any action. Returning to the courthouse situation, a proposition supporting the status quo would be the equivalent of an un-accused person appearing in court to plead his or her innocence when, in fact, the individual has not been charged with any wrongdoing.

In practice, determining the proposition then is a matter of assessing which side you are on, and this is a critical step in determining your argumentative responsibilities or "burdens." As you will learn in the next chapter, the side advocating change, like the prosecutor, has greater responsibilities than advocates of the status quo. Either way, understanding which side you are on begins with identifying the proposition.

4. A proposition provides room for both sides to argue

The proposition is *not* a persuasive device used to influence how audiences feel about one or the other side of the issue but is an instrument that helps the advocate better understand the nature of the disagreement. An effort to explain the controversy in a neutral way will require you to transcend the argument – to try to remove yourself from the controversy and to think of it in an unbiased way. Transcending the argument means being mindful of the fact that the language and terminology you use in a public controversy will reflect bias, intentional or not, toward your own points of view. For most, neutrality in writing a proposition in a fair and balanced manner is a matter of language and terminology. For example, what one side of the controversy over the Affordable Care Act terms a "government takeover of medicine," the other side describes as "universal access to healthcare." Attempts to neutrally describe this controversy in a proposition usually involve learning enough about the public issue to understand where the true lines of controversy are drawn and selecting language and terminology that are not inherently evocative of support for one side or the other. Others may launch into advocacy when the task is intended to be limited to constructing an accurate and fairly worded assessment of the controversy. An example of a proposition that overreaches is something like, "The U.S. federal government should legalize marijuana because the drug trade is leading to the murder of thousands of innocent Mexican citizens." That the drug trade in America is causing the murder of thousands of innocent Mexican citizens is an argument the change advocate might make in favor of the proposition; it has no place in the proposition itself. The easiest way to check for this form of overreach is to look for the term "because" or something similar. If this type of extended explanation is present, there is likely overreach.

Propositions in Ongoing Controversies

The ability to identify propositions accurately is important for advocates and target audiences. During a controversy over a proposal to change the status quo, many arguments pertaining to an unstated proposition may be disputed. As a consequence, untrained advocates may, as it is said, fail to "see the forest for the trees." Recognizing a controversy and understanding precisely where sides oppose each other allow you to understand where *you* are entering the controversy, as well as the implications of your advocacy on the larger proposition. This allows you to answer the question, "What is my contribution to this controversy?"

The controversy over federal ethanol subsidies helps us illustrate these points. Ethanol is a fuel produced from fermented corn. To fund the process, corn farmers receive a great deal of financial assistance from the federal government so they can affordably grow enough corn. People researching this topic will find public essays, op-eds, and statements from politicians and think tanks, among other sources, discussing whether there is a need for ethanol, if we should produce more ethanol, whether refineries should be mandated to blend more ethanol with gasoline, whether ethanol consumes more energy in production than it produces, whether ethanol harms engines, whether support exists because of the powerful farmers' lobby, and whether ethanol production drives up other food costs. Any one piece read in isolation from the others or without a firm grasp of the proposition can prevent the reader from understanding how the information or opinion expressed in an individual news item or opinion column matters to the larger argument. While the thesis of each piece contributes somehow to the larger proposition, it is imperative to understand the way in which it does. For instance, if it is a true fact that ethanol harms engines, then ethanol may be more harmful than beneficial. If that is the case, then this fact has important implications for the larger controversy. After substantial consideration of these matters, you would likely determine that the proposition is something like the following: "The U.S. federal government should end ethanol subsidies."

Consider another example; for more than a year, the Obama administration and its supporters advocated for various elements of its healthcare position by employing numerous argumentative strategies. Meanwhile, they were rebutting their opponents' arguments against the Affordable Care Act. As the legislation wound its way through committees, the U.S. Senate, the House of Representatives, and the White House, proponents of the legislation tried to manage public attitudes in favor of the act. During that campaign, Princeton economist Paul Krugman published a *New York Times* op-ed piece titled, "Fear Strikes Out," in which he compared President Obama's appeals aimed at the House of Representatives to pass the Affordable Care Act to the fearful tenor of Newt Gingrich's arguments against the legislation.[2] This op-ed did not clearly advocate for the proposition, "The U.S. Congress should adopt the Affordable Care Act," nor did it indirectly give substantive reasons to support the proposed act. On its own, Krugman's thesis is that the president's healthcare rhetoric was more consistent with American optimism than was the rhetoric of his opponents. Employing what you know about the context, however, you can recognize this op-ed fitting into the larger campaign supporting the legislation. Using your knowledge of the ongoing debate at the time, you could maintain Krugman is "affirming" the proposition. And once this proposition is ascertained by readers, they can assess whether the evidence and reasoning used by Krugman provides reasons for believing the legislation should be adopted.

In any advocacy event, people will only listen to so much for so long. As such, each element of a deliberative argument cannot be included each time an advocate voices an opinion about a subject. To adapt, arguers such as Krugman must be able to contribute to the argument without addressing the entire proposition. Far from merely offering his summary of the issue, Krugman is criticizing opponents of the Affordable Care Act as dishonest and unmoved by evidence. This calls into question the level of confidence the public should accord arguments used by the opponents of the Affordable Care Act. Though the scope of his argument is very narrow, vis-à-vis the larger argument, it has clear implications for the larger proposition.

Types of Propositions

Controversies can differ both according to their subject matter as well as their scope (or how broad or narrow the dispute is). Regarding the scope of a controversy, it is useful to ask, what is the nature of what you are asking your audience to agree with? Do you want them to believe that something is true (or false), that something is good (or bad), or that something should be done (or not done)? These three questions represent three different types of controversies. The first is termed a question (or proposition) of fact – a dispute about whether something is or is not true. The second is a question (or proposition) of value – an evaluation of some activity, behavior, or action according to some value (whether some action is good or bad is the easiest way to think about value questions). The last is the focus of this book – a question (or proposition) of policy. Each type of controversy differs according to what does and does not pertain to the dispute, and so for each type of controversy a different proposition is warranted.

Propositions of Fact and Value

In propositions of fact, advocates are contending that something is or is not true. *Social Security is headed toward bankruptcy. Global warming is caused by fossil fuels. The United States did not land astronauts on the moon.* Each of these claims is either true or false. These are narrow factual disputes, relative to value and policy arguments. Consider the following hypothetical argument in which you maintain that marijuana helps combat wasting disease, a side effect of late-stage cancers and AIDS that literally causes the sufferer to "waste away." In this instance, your proposition is, "Marijuana helps combat the harms of wasting disease in terminally ill patients." If in response your friend replies, "But marijuana is bad," his or her point would be beyond the scope of your factual proposition. All things considered, marijuana may be "bad." In this instance, however, you are not considering all things – just if marijuana has the claimed effects. In the end, the value of knowing that the core of your dispute is strictly limited to the veracity of a factual claim is to help you avoid the distraction of irrelevant assertions that may not challenge your or another's factual proposition. At times it is useful for advocates to limit themselves to making just factual claims.

Propositions of value, on the other hand, are arguments about the *value* of something. *Social Security is a social good. The war in Afghanistan is unethical. Violence is a justified response to political oppression.* These are value propositions, and value propositions include more within their boundaries than do propositions of fact because they involve both matters of value *and* fact. Realizing the role of factual matters in value claims prepares you to recognize the sub-arguments that must be addressed if you are to successfully argue a value proposition: In the case of a basic good/bad proposition, you must argue both that something *is* and that it is *good* or *bad*. For instance, if arguing, "Social Security is bad," your argument is going to be stronger if facts are established about the program's harms before an overall evaluation of Social Security is developed in your argument. Factual sub-arguments of this value proposition may focus on Social Security's pending bankruptcy, that it redistributes money from the wealthy and employed to retired Americans, that it inadequately provides for poor retirees, or that its payments fail to keep up with inflation. Once these matters of fact are established, the advocate can move on to assessing the activity under consideration according to some value.

Considering the earlier argument about marijuana: if your friend asserts that "Marijuana is bad," and you choose to challenge his or her assertion, you have effectively chosen to entertain a larger dispute; the proposition around which your dispute centers has changed. You are no longer arguing only about the veracity of facts but have moved onto *evaluating* those facts. Perhaps your friend concedes the assertion that marijuana helps combat wasting disease; he or she has not necessarily conceded that marijuana is good, just that it has these effects. Though they may often seem to be, facts are not by themselves good or bad, which is why value determinations constitute their own type of proposition.

Regarding the proposition that "Marijuana is bad," your friend might make factual sub-arguments establishing marijuana's harmful effects; let us picture him or her describing it as a gateway drug that functions as a stepping-stone to a life of drug dependency and premature death. There are two arguments here. First, the factual sub-argument establishes facts that link marijuana use to drug dependency and premature death. Second, he or she has to make the rather easy, in this case, value argument that drug dependency and premature death are bad. In the real world, those maintaining that marijuana use is bad rarely have a problem with the value component of the argument, as few are willing to counter that drug dependency and premature death are good or neutral consequences. Instead, marijuana's opponents struggle to establish the *factual* sub-arguments that link marijuana to these harmful outcomes.

Propositions of value involve the value systems of arguers and their audiences. While speakers and audiences may have similar value systems, quite often they differ. Different parties may often disagree about values or prioritize their values differently. In cases like these, arguments need to be made that illumine the values undergirding claims and promote the primacy of such values. For example, imagine a pundit on a news talk show arguing that sweatshops employing low-paid and young workers in foreign countries are good, without much further explanation. The value argument is poorly developed, and so video clips of the statement circulate on political websites showing how "heartless" or "out of touch" the advocate is. Had the pundit explained the value position from which these facts were to be evaluated, viewers may have drawn a different conclusion about him or her. Later, he or she may explain that he or she values greater economic opportunity for the workers and claim that nations where such factories are located are in an early, but necessary, stages of economic development. In contrast, Barack Obama's healthcare appeals often involved relatively more explicit value arguments focused on compassion, fairness, and empathy for families without healthcare coverage. The president's often-used line, "We are our brother's keeper," is a value argument cribbed from the Bible reminding the audience of values that place empathy and selflessness over self-interest or order.

Propositions of Policy

Propositions of policy concern whether something should or should not be done and are the primary focus of this book, because it is around matters of policy that most public argument centers. *The U.S. federal government should privatize Social Security. The federal government should reduce fossil fuel consumption. The United States should withdraw its military from Afghanistan.* These propositions affirm a change to the status quo, as all policy propositions do. Furthermore, each identifies an agent of action and the goal the advocate has for the agent. The boundaries of policy arguments are the most expansive of the three types of propositions; in addition to any policy argument, both facts and values will be disputed.

A strong appeal supporting a public policy proposition will establish facts about the status quo, evaluate those facts, and outline changes to the system that will remedy the problem revealed by the facts. Returning to the marijuana argument with your friend, if you state, "Marijuana should be legalized," you have initiated a *policy* argument that includes fact and value sub-arguments. To be successfull with this argument, you will have to establish that there is a need that is not being met (a factual claim). You may argue that young people charged with misdemeanor marijuana possession lose the right to vote and describe the extent of the costs of law enforcement, litigation, and corrections. You may also address matters of value, arguing that losing the right to vote for such a minor infraction runs counter to values that you and your friend hold and that the expense of the status quo far outweighs the advantages of prohibiting, or penalizing, marijuana use. This establishes that a change is needed. When you begin to advocate for a change to the status quo, the argument has moved beyond matters of fact and value into the realm of policy advocacy.

Because deliberative argument deals with the future, the reliability of facts used to predict outcomes is especially important. *Will the Affordable Care Act make healthcare more affordable? Will ending federal support for ethanol save the nation money? Will tax cuts cause the economy to grow?* You can never know with certainty what the outcomes of policies will be. Still, deliberating about the future is certainly better than relying on whims of tradition or edicts of dictators. Public policy advocacy exposes reasoning and evidence to scrutiny. Where do the facts come from? Who collected them? Why were they collected? Are they trustworthy? Are they consistent with other facts? Whether or not facts are true is extremely important, because the outcomes of public policy advocacy and subsequent policy decisions often hinge on these facts. For instance, if it can be factually shown that tax cuts have contributed to a nation's economic growth in the *past*, you might reasonably conclude that cutting taxes can stimulate the economy in the *future*. Asking hypothetically, "Do tax cuts *contribute* to economic growth?" reveals how and why facts become controversial. Disputes about facts are often the foundation of any deliberative argument.

In the next chapter, we consider what are referred to as "stock issues" in policy argumentation.

Exercise 2: Proposition Recognition Assignment

You are to identify the proposition operating within a current public controversy. If you completed Exercise 1, you are encouraged to use the same issue for this assignment. From the material you are examining, select one editorial, or extended blog posting, or other primary document from the controversy. Identify the proposition the writer is addressing. Keep in mind the writer may never state the proposition and/or may be opposed to the proposition. Develop a sentence for the proposition consistent with the four requirements outlined in this chapter. Then identify which side the writer is on. Is he or she a proponent of the proposition or an opponent? As far as you can tell, what are the reasons the writer believes the proposition should or should not be supported?

Notes

1. Robert Huber and Alfred C. Snider, *Influencing through Argument* (New York: International Debate Education Association, 2006), 15.
2. Paul Krugman, "Fear Strikes Out," *New York Times*, March 21, 2010. Accessed September 15, 2013, http://www.nytimes.com/2010/03/22/opinion/22krugman.html.

· 3 ·

UNDERSTANDING STOCK ISSUES IN PUBLIC POLICY ADVOCACY

Takeaways

1. Stock issues are matters of potential dispute that bear on the proposition (that there is a problem, a cause of that problem, a possible solution, and that advantages will accompany that solution). Initially these are burdens of advocates affirming the propositions – affirmative advocates. Advocates negating the proposition – negative advocates – must also hold affirmative advocates responsible for providing these components of a policy proposal.
2. Knowledge of the stock issues helps you scrutinize advocacy (your own or others') by directing your attention to these key components and the reasoning and evidence used to support them. All public policy controversies involve stock issues whether or not they are explicitly discussed.
3. Because public policy controversies are often long-term efforts, it is unlikely that all stock issues will be specifically addressed in a given advocacy event. You must use your knowledge of the larger controversy to understand the extent to which information satisfies argumentative burdens.

Introduction

Once the proposition is identified, additional analysis of a public controversy is informed by the identification of what are commonly referred to as "stock issues." Stock issues are matters of potential disagreement that are "stock" or standard for a type of proposition. If you are challenging the status quo in a public policy environment, stock issues are required parts of the arguments that affirm a policy proposition. If you are defending the status quo, stock issues function as a template, directing your attention to content that should be present in the argument of the advocate calling for change. This chapter discusses stock issues and their role in the actual practice of public policy advocacy. Knowledge of stock issues will equip you to evaluate the presence, strength, and weakness of arguments you and others are expected to make in pursuit of good policy. Knowledge of stock issues also assists in understanding where the arguments you and others make fit into the larger controversy within which minor or isolated claims are asserted.

Stock Issues: The Anatomy of Public Policy Advocacy

Stock issues provide a detailed system for understanding the standard components of public policy advocacy. Public policy disputes, whether factual or evaluative, most often center on the following matters:

a. **Problem:** A description of the significant harms that need to be remedied.
b. **Cause:** A description of the cause of the harms.
c. **Solution:** A workable proposal that will remove the problem.
d. **Advantages:** A description of the advantages that result from the solution.

In practice, all four of these items are unlikely to be expressed in any one public appeal, and yet all four of these issues have bearing on any matter of policy. Knowing these issues and being prepared to argue them are responsibilities of advocates seeking either to change or maintain the status quo.

This book has already introduced the idea that the status quo is "presumed innocent" in a public argument; that is, the status quo is presumed to be sufficient and not in need of change. Starting here, we will use typical academic debate terminology to describe the two sides of the public "debate," referring to "affirmative" advocates and "negative" advocates. *Affirmatives* seek to change the status quo. *Negatives* seek to defend the status quo.

The Burdens of Advocacy

Stock issues are initially matters of importance for affirmative advocates, but once affirmative advocates outline their concern with the status quo, stock issues become useful for negative advocates. Stock issues outline what amounts to a weighty task: the target audience must be convinced of the affirmative advocate's position on all four issues. As such, affirmative advocates begin the argument and seek to argue all four stock issues convincingly; negative advocates engage in refutation that addresses the stock issues in an effort to convince the audience that the affirmative's analysis is flawed. During a public controversy, it is rare for all four stock issues to be addressed in any one advocacy event. Few official public forums would allow advocates to speak for such an extended period of time, although written formats might permit the submission of briefs, opinion papers, or memoranda that permit a fuller presentation and refutation associated with the stock issues. In many advocacy settings, your audience will understand that you are providing only a part of a larger presentation and assume that you would be able to provide more material if it was requested. It is useful in this regard to think of a case made by an affirmative as similar to a house; you see the front of the house and assume the sides and back of the house are there. As with a house, the mind will typically assume a complete argument exists without you having to reiterate all of its key components. However, the negative advocate will likely upset this mental process, calling on the audience to look more closely for each component and the soundness of the affirmative position overall.

Problem

Similar to a defendant who is presumed innocent in a courtroom until a convincing case for guilt can be made, advocates can safely assume the public is inclined to view the status quo as sufficient. This assumption might figure the public as indifferent about issues because they are either unaware of the problem or the problem is perceived as insignificant, remote, unchangeable, or too costly to change. The first responsibility of the affirmative advocate then is to impress upon the public that the concern they wish to address is significantly harmful to warrant the public's attention. The point at which a problem is harmful enough to address is purely subjective – it depends on the problem and the target audience. Convincing the public that federal action is needed to regulate parasailing is going to be more challenging than convincing the public of the need to evacuate an expectant volcano's blast zone. To convince an audience of a problem's significance, the advocate must possess knowledge of the extent of the problem and/or vivid descriptions of the potential or actual harm.

Consider again the Affordable Care Act. The Democratic Party invested a tremendous amount of effort building public support for the Affordable Care Act. Town hall meetings were held by members of Congress; the President went on a speaking tour as well as television interviews; and advocacy advertisements were aired. Many of these efforts were crafted to educate Americans of the extent of the problem, with statistics showing millions without access to healthcare facing bankruptcy in the event of an illness requiring medical attention, and heart-wrenching stories of individuals who avoided medical attention in order to save money, only to suffer irreversible pain and suffering or death. In the end, the Obama Administration described a compelling problem.

Sometimes the problem is described as a "need," because the problem is better cast as an impending dilemma, an imperfection that will escalate over time and present society with serious consequences worth avoiding if possible. The greater the perceived need, the stronger the desire will be among the public for a solution. If an advocate fails to convince the audience of a problem's significance, the audience will not perceive need enough to support a change. This is well illustrated by President George W. Bush's efforts to privatize Social Security. Bush toured the country, hosting town hall events at which he made his case for privatization. In the final analysis, however, neither the people nor Congress were convinced of the need to change the Social Security system. Congress never even voted on it.

If you are an affirmative advocate, you must argue persuasively that a need exists to solve a problem. Problems can range from concerns about workplace unfairness to genocide. Fortunately, problems do not need to rise to the level of genocide killings to warrant change to the status quo. How significant a problem must be to warrant a change is up to the subjective judgment of the target audience. The perceived relevance of a problem to the target audience is one factor. Additionally, problems can be measured quantitatively or qualitatively. Quantitative measures can, for example, demonstrate how widespread a problem is. You could establish the housing foreclosure crisis as a significant problem by numerically showing the large number of homes that have been foreclosed or are in foreclosure, are "under water" (worth less than what is still owed to the lender), or have been "short sold" (being sold for less than is owed), and how these failing mortgages and desperate acts affect large numbers of families and lenders. Skillfully communicated, with graphics or verbal comparisons, these numbers can be perceived as significant enough to warrant change.

Sometimes, quantitative measures of problems are not enough to generate a perceived need. A large problem may have been part of our awareness for so long that it is perceived as acceptable or simply "the way things are." World-wide, people suffer from hunger and political oppression, and yet many people do nothing about it, either individually or as a society. What if a billion people worldwide suffer from hunger? Would such a number motivate the citizens of nations with ample food supply to seek a solution to the problem? Problems such as these, for many, are too remote or abstract. In such cases, qualitative measures may be far more compelling. Television advertisements appealing to U.S. residents to give money to help the world's impoverished do not limit their arguments to numerical assessments of the problem's size, if they mention its size at all. Including so many hungry, poorly clothed, and seemingly unhealthy children in their advertisements, these images tug at viewers' heart-strings and can be far more powerful as persuasive tools than statistics could ever be. Because an injustice affects someone else, getting an audience to perceive it as a significant problem can be challenging. A qualitative description of it, however, can trigger the empathy and sympathy of a target audience.

Cause

The source of a problem is its cause. If you are an affirmative advocate, your advocacy efforts should include an earnest effort to identify the cause. This is both a practical and ethical burden. The failure to identify the correct source of the problem when developing and advocating a solution can result in – fig-uratively – putting a band-aid over a gunshot wound. While the bandage may have the short-term effect of making society feel like it has remedied a prob-lem, in the long-run, this failure may be wasteful and distracting and may pro-long or exacerbate the problem. Worse, failure to identify the correct source of the problem can lead to no relief, temporary or otherwise. The identification of the cause follows discussion of the problem because, ideally, the stock issue of problem conditions the target audience to seek a solution and prepares the audience to recognize the fitness of the solution.

We maintain that arguing cause as a separate issue is a responsibility of an advocate who seeks to enact good policy. Policymakers are often criticized, sometimes harshly and for long periods of time, for failing to appropriately support, or demand appropriate support for, the identified cause. A common scenario for this criticism is to allege that a particularly awful event (described as the problem), or other activity that causes outrage, permits advocates to identify a cause, or ignore altogether the question of cause, without much pushback or scrutiny. The public discussion about the causes of the 9/11 attacks on the World Trade Center and the eventual decision of the U.S. government to invade Iraq as part of the "War on Terror" is a commonly referenced example of a failure to properly scrutinize an alleged cause. Frightened by the perception of extremist Islamic animosity toward the United States following the 9/11 attacks in New York, critics argue, decision makers accepted the invasion of Iraq as part of a solution to protect the United States from another attack. Iraq possessed one of the least religious governments in the Muslim world and had no demonstrable link to the attacks, and evidence supporting its alleged possession of weapons of mass destruction (and probable use of them against the United States) was highly suspect. In other words, critics claim there was insufficient evidence to support the notion that Iraq was part of the cause of the 9/11 attacks or constituted an imminent threat to the United States. The pre-emptive invasion arguably helped spawn disdain for the United States among Muslims in Iraq and its neighboring nations. Because good public policy advocacy should invite scrutiny, a careful examination of cause in this instance should have taken place. The public's appreciation of the stock issue of cause could have been the impetus for generating a public discussion of the Bush Administration's Iraq-as-cause assertion. Ultimately, the United States spent over $1 trillion, over 4,400 U.S. soldiers have died, over 32,000 U.S. soldiers have been wounded, and hundreds of thousands of Iraqi citizens have perished.[1]

Even where there is no outrage, often advocates do not concern themselves with an analysis of the cause. This may be due to the time limitations of an advocacy event, and it may simply occur because an advocate assumes his or her audience is of like mind on cause. Advocates may ignore the identification of the cause, expecting that the audience will fill in the blank (a phenomenon we discuss in more detail in chapter four's discussion of the "enthymeme," or incomplete argument). On a practical level, for affirmative advocates the takeaway is that the particular controversy or advocacy setting may not always require the identification and discussion of cause; however, the potential for flawed policymaking should offer you ample motivation to consider cause in the development of the solution, and always be prepared to address it.

How you define the cause is critical to whether you can convince an audience your solution will address the problem. Argument scholar Lee Hultzen uses the term "reformability" instead of cause to name this stock issue.[2] His choice of language captures an important facet of cause as a stock issue – that some problems are defined in ways that make reform impossible. An affirmative advocate's job is to convince the audience that the cause of the problem can be effectively addressed. But no public policy can stop hurricanes, floods, or volcanoes, for instance. Problems caused by hurricanes, however, are a product of flooding and wind damage, not hurricanes per se. Thus the cause could focus on reformable conditions, permitting solutions that, for example, address flooding and wind damage (moving people from flood prone areas, strengthening building codes, etc.). You are perhaps familiar with this quandary as it appears in discussion of the problem of poverty. Advocates who isolate the cause of poverty to be inadequate education claim the cause is reformable. Advocates who isolate the cause of poverty as laziness claim the cause is not reformable.

Advocates may find useful another system of analysis for describing the extent to which aspects of the status quo contribute to (that is, cause) the problem's present existence. This system, sometimes referred to as "inherency analysis," considers four common barriers to the enactment of a satisfactory solution to the problem.[3] Those barriers are structural, attitudinal, philosophical, and existential conditions that, advocates claim, are inherent to the status quo. As a skilled advocate, you should understand these claimed barriers because they help you understand the relationship, or lack of, between the problem and the proposed solution. Understanding inherency also enables you to assess the potential effectiveness of a proposed solution, whether it can overcome the barriers within the status quo that bear on the problem as it has been described. Barriers are typically presented as part of the direct cause of the problem or something that is preventing the status quo from correcting itself.

Structural barriers are systemic realities that prevent the status quo from solving the problem on its own. You should ask, what structures are in place that support the continuation of the problem, and is there a solution that can overcome these structural barriers? Consider efforts to solve the Recession of 2008. Many argued that what prevented economic recovery was a structural barrier: people did not have enough spending money and programs such as extended unemployment benefits, public aid, and government spending on infrastructure improvements were not being supported by policymakers. In this case, lack of government intervention (a solution) and the opponents of such intervention were structural barriers. Opponents of government intervention, on the other hand, believed the system would self-correct. Many economic conservatives believe that economic recessions are self-correcting problems that do not require government intervention. They argue that economic recessions lead to a drop in the cost of borrowing money for businesses and families, thus encouraging consumer spending and spurring investment in new production. Layoffs drive labor prices down, they maintain, which spurs new hiring because employers can afford more labor. Now, according to this perspective, more people would see their earnings rise and prices would decline, triggering new economic growth. If this is true, does the government need to enact a stimulus plan to encourage growth and production? Economic conservatives say no. They claim that there is no barrier inherent to the status quo that is preventing the problem from going away on its own.

Attitudinal barriers prevent the status quo from self-correcting by way of attitudes, feelings, or opinions held by the people who are perpetuating the problem. Attitudes are trickier for you to address because the system cannot just legislate attitude. You should consider what attitudes are in place that support the continuation of the problem and whether there is a solution that can overcome these attitudinal barriers. In many public transactions, discrimination based on race, whether or not it is intended, is illegal. Real estate transactions are one such transaction in which discrimination against people of a specific race or ethnicity is punishable. Nevertheless, the law cannot eliminate bias in these transactions because they are caused by attitudes, and the presence of such attitudes is not always clearly evident. Thus, the extent to which real estate discrimination can be further reduced depends on whether attitudes can be changed.

When predominantly held values, truths, or philosophies prevent your solution from being adopted, it is said to be blocked by a *philosophical barrier*. While identifying this barrier does not help explain the strengths or flaws of your policy proposal, awareness of such a barrier magnifies the value of public policy advocacy in promoting your solution. Because it is the audience's hierarchy of values, or philosophy, that needs to be overcome or reprioritized, they'll need convincing of that.

In the practice of public advocacy, causes cannot always be identified. Moreover, a persuasive case for a policy change does not always allow for, or necessitate the identification of, the problem's cause. After establishing that a significant problem either has not historically solved itself or demands immediate action, your advocacy may proceed with the built-in assumption that a cause exists, regardless of whether you have identified it. In such a case, an *existential barrier* is said to exist, which is to merely acknowledge that a barrier *exists* and a solution must be adopted regardless of whether the cause is known. Consider the social ill of poverty (a problem). Poverty is not caused by the failure of the government to give away free money, but malnutrition is caused by the inability to purchase food. Though, in theory, advocates may never know if the status quo could have solved the problem on its own, they may not be willing to risk the untimely deaths of millions of poor adults and children to find out.

Good critical thinkers will question whether the *entire* cause has been identified or if the cause that has been identified works in combination with other contributing factors. Will addressing one structural barrier, for example, eradicate the problem at all if other factors are also responsible? Will removing one of many barriers simply reduce the problem, and if so, will the amount of reduction of the problem be worth the cost of the solution? These are questions worthy of consideration by both affirmative and negative advocates. This is particularly true because affirmative advocates will tout the achievements of their remedy, even if it addresses a small portion of the problem they set out to solve. Consider again the matter of poverty. If the problem that public assistance is intended to solve is poor nutrition, it will likely solve much of that problem. However, if the problem laid out in the public argument is poverty itself, then public assistance is likely to have limited effectiveness in addressing that problem. If studies show that the root causes of poverty are a lack of skills and ignorance about financial management, giving people money will not address those causes, though it may alleviate some of poverty's consequences, and that may be enough of a gain to warrant the adoption of the solution.

Solution

Training in academic debate instructs the student to develop a very detailed solution, particularly when a plan is complex. The components of a plan are often referred to as "planks," and generally, there are four such planks: agency, mandates, funding mechanism, and enforcement mechanism. These planks are a good starting point for policymaking because they direct the affirmative advocate to begin the development of policy by addressing the four most substantial matters of policy. Both the nature of the plan and the circumstances of the advocacy event determine what the advocate needs to include. There are some situations in which no plan is needed at all. For example, if the affirmative advocate argues that discrimination against gays and lesbians was caused by the Defense of Marriage Act, then the proposal is, quite simply, the repeal of that law. An example of a public argument that necessitated a more detailed plan, however, is the Affordable Care Act. The Affordable Care Act consists of 955 total pages outlining new agencies, mandates, taxes, and enforcement mechanisms. No public forum exists, however, that would withstand a thorough description of this legislation. The affirmative advocate, then, is left to decide what parts of the proposed solution to explain in detail. How does the advocate whittle 955 pages of legislation down to a manageable speech or op-ed piece? What follows is a brief consideration of how to reconcile complex solutions with the public's need to consider all of its merits.

Agency

The agency is a description of what apparatus will implement and administer the solution. The proposed agency, government or private insurers, attracted serious attention during the public debate about the Affordable Care Act. Democrats seeking to solve the problem of people without healthcare coverage debated the issue of agency before proposing their solution. Some believed a government-run or "single-payer" plan would work best, while others thought private insurers would be better. The single-payer option would have had the government take over the entire health insurance industry, making it the single or only agency compensating doctors for their work. Instead, the Affordable Care Act proposed a plan that used the private insurance markets as the agency of health insurance coverage; private insurance companies would continue to provide healthcare coverage. In this case, publicly identifying the agency was important in order to pre-empt anticipated counter-arguments made by negative advocates warning against "government takeovers" of "one sixth of the nation's economy," or "socialism."

The design of the Affordable Care Act puts a fine point on the importance of the agency plank in public policy advocacy. In the present political environment, there is a great deal of distrust about the ability of government bureaucracies to solve problems. This was likely factored into the solution's design in order to help avoid opposition. Agency, as well as the other planks, need to be more than workable; they must be acceptable.

These are two different matters, and acceptability, in particular, is a matter of audience attitudes and perhaps also philosophical principles, such as that the free market will offer the most effective means of reducing the costs of healthcare.

Mandates

Mandates are descriptions of authority and directives given to agencies to execute a policy. Banks, for instance, are mandated by the federal government to report deposits in excess of $10,000 to the Internal Revenue Service (IRS). Arizona's controversial immigration law mandates that documented immigrants must carry their federal registration documents at all times. The Affordable Care Act's 955-page healthcare bill has more mandates than can be described in any public message. There are two key mandates in the legislation. First, the legislation requires people to purchase private health insurance, similar to the way states require drivers to purchase automobile insurance. Second, the legislation requires states to set up Internet-based "exchanges," or sites, that allow insurance shoppers to compare prices for similar levels of coverage offered by different insurance companies. Advocates need to balance a number of factors when deciding what and how to describe the mandates in their plan. What are the mandates? How many are there? How complex are they? How does or will the public perceive the mandates? How does the opposition perceive the mandates?

Funding

The affirmative advocate's discussion of funding is an explanation of how the plan's execution will be funded. Even a proposal as simple as allowing gays and lesbians to marry has a cost; more people will qualify for spousal Social Security benefits and tax deductions, for instance, resulting in less federal revenue. Funding for the Affordable Care Act became a very important point of contention during the debate that led to its adoption, and it continues to generate concern from opponents of the law. The requirement to purchase health insurance obligates the federal government to subsidize the insurance purchases for those in need. This is funded, in part, by a number of specific tax increases, including a "sin tax" on tanning beds. Anticipating resistance to the proposal of new spending and tax increases, the Obama administration made an argument that was complex – that the trajectory of the present healthcare system was going to make current federal healthcare obligations an unaffordable burden and that the status quo (before adoption of the law) would become more expensive when compared to the proposed changes. Thus it was reasoned that more involvement by the government in this industry (usually associated with greater costs) would help reduce predicted cost increases. The new law, claimed its proponents, would cost money, but it would also result in savings elsewhere (i.e., lower cost projections for Medicare and Medicaid).

When we teach argumentation and debate in class, we instruct students to propose raising taxes – that, if a problem is worth solving and the solution is effective, the affirmative advocate should not hesitate to propose a tax increase or assess a fee. Student hesitance to propose tax increases, even in an artificial debate setting, reflects the strength with which opposition to taxes is held by most of the public. This attitude affects both public argument and how public policy is crafted. Some advocates will not even use the word "tax," preferring to say "revenue enhancement" and "contributions." Clearly, affirmative advocates must proceed with caution when discussing any solution that requires funding.

Knowledge of the affirmative's responsibility to describe a funding mechanism gives the negative advocate a valuable tool. Not only are many audiences averse to increased taxes, but the negative can make a strong argument that a plan without a funding mechanism produces no benefits. Advantages cannot be derived from an unfunded mandate. Imagine if your town mandated that each home participate in the recycling pickup program. Residents would be required to sort and place recyclable waste at their curb on Wednesdays. The town, however, failed to provide any money to hire a waste management firm to collect the recyclables. Recycling advocates may be right about the general benefits of recycling, but they would be wrong to argue that your town's mandate would produce benefits absent a funding mechanism.

Enforcement

Enforcement mechanisms are means by which the mandates are executed. African American citizens were guaranteed the right to vote in 1870 by the Fifteenth Amendment, but these rights were not fully realized, particularly in southern states, until the mid-twentieth century because the federal government refused to enforce it. The Supreme Court's decision that segregation was unconstitutional was meaningless until President Eisenhower ordered the 101st Airborne Division of the U.S. Army to escort the Little Rock Nine into an Arkansas high school in 1957. Desegregation efforts and civil rights laws are of little value if they cannot be enforced.

After the Affordable Care Act was passed, the enforcement mechanism became the centerpiece of the opposition's argument. If the success of the legislation hinges on a requirement to buy health insurance, how do you force people to buy health insurance? The government proposed enforcing this rule by having the IRS charge a penalty, theoretically removing any incentive to avoid the purchase. Several states later challenged the constitutionality of requiring citizens to buy *anything*. During the summer of 2012, the Supreme Court issued its *National Federation of Independent Business v. Sebelius* decision, indicating that the penalty was actually a tax, deeming it constitutional under the government's authority to levy taxes. Sometimes the enforcement mechanism is the most complex or controversial part of the plan. If the U.S. Constitution is ever amended to ban abortion, how will that be enforced? By the time *Roe v. Wade* was decided by the Supreme Court, nearly a million abortions were performed each year, the vast majority of which were illegal. Clearly, state laws banning abortions at the time, regardless of the support they may have had within their respective states, included enforcement mechanism that were deemed undesirable.

The affirmative advocate's discussion of enforcement in public argument is important because it ensures that the proposed solution will be executed. The public, convinced of the need to solve a problem and poised to pay for the solution, will want assurance that the proposal will work as planned. Whether a detailed description of an enforcement mechanism is necessary often depends on the solution and the challenges raised by the opposition. An affirmative advocate should always be prepared to discuss the enforcement mechanism when it is relevant to the solution.

Unlike academic debate, how one best publicly discusses policy specifics is an art and involves a large number of choices. Thinking back on the public controversy about the Affordable Care Act, in no one public presentation, spoken or written, were all of these four planks outlined. Doing so would be neither feasible nor tolerable in most advocacy settings. Some of it may be above the public's technical capacity to comprehend. Adequately explaining each of these planks, however, in the event that the advocate needs to, helps avoid counter-arguments maintaining that the solution is not workable. Disagreements about a solution's workability emerge (a) if the opposition maintains that the affirmative advocate has not made clear how the plan will work or (b) if the opposition has evidence the plan will not work.

It is in a discussion of workability that we ought to address the notion of "fiat," or the theoretical idea that the purpose of policy debate is to assess the merits of a proposed plan, not the political feasibility of passing the proposed solution through a legislative body or other such practical matters that might suggest the solution would never come into existence. "Will the Affordable Care Act produce the desired advantages?" is a question for policy debate, while "Will Congress actually pass the Affordable Care Act?" is not. The second question is just political forecasting, and the outcome of a discussion so focused would reveal nothing about the legislation's merits. Fiat plays less of a role in public policy advocacy, however, because questions of political feasibility may be legitimate audience concerns. We are not suggesting that feasibility questions should be confused with questions about a solution's workability. Instead, the advocate must be prepared to address feasibility. For example, while there has been a great deal of discussion in the United States about immigration reform, congressional Republicans have made clear that they will not discuss so-called pathways to citizenship for immigrants who entered the country illegally. The refusal to consider pathways to citizenship has little to do with evidence-based consideration of its outcomes (will pathways to citizenship fail to produce advantages?). Instead, many Republicans are concerned about primary challenges from conservatives within their own party (will passing pathways to citizenship anger party leadership, donors, and voters?). Nevertheless, while fiat may play less of a role in public policy advocacy, a public policy advocate must be discerning enough to distinguish between matters of plan workability and political feasibility, if only to point out the opposition's avoidance of debate over a proposal's merits.

Advantages

The stock issue of advantages addresses the problems the solution aims to solve and may also include multiple advantages. Advantages perform two functions: first, they demonstrate that the plan fulfills its intended purpose of fixing the harm (this is also termed "solvency"); second, a rhetorical function, they provide a description of the solution that intensifies audience desire for it. While it seems logical that a workable solution that solves a significant problem is desirable all on its own, simply showing solvency can limit the persuasiveness of your appeal. This is the reason why it is rhetorically advantageous to highlight advantages; it is where the advocate gets to describe the good things that come from the solution.

The academic debate student is trained to show solvency in a systematic way. Solvency is the affirmative advocate's demonstration that the problems warranting a change to the status quo are solved by the proposal. If, for instance, two significant problems are outlined in the affirmative advocate's argument, both should be solved or reduced in the solution step. Take, for instance, arguments about public schools. Many people agree that poor academic performance and high dropout rates are problems with American high schools.

Significant problems exist with the nation's high schools.

A. High school academic performance is too low.
B. High school dropout rates are too high.

If an advocate promotes a solution for these problems, the solution should be shown to fix both. Because it is assumed that an advocate would, if he or she could, show that a solution is likely to solve cited problems, failure to give reasons to believe that a reduction or eradication of cited problems is likely might reasonably suggest that one of them was included just to scare the audience into accepting the proposed solution. In this case, solvency is an argument demonstrating that the solution improves performance *and* reduces dropouts.

The proposed solution reduces the problems.

A. The solution will improve high school academic performance.
B. The solution will reduce high school dropout rates.

Thus, each problem affirmative advocates outline would need to be either solved or reduced. Reasons to believe that the proposal will have each intended effect, and on a scale that justifies the effort, should be the affirmative advocate's objective.

There are important technical elements of advantages that should be used when developing public policy advocacy. First, addressing in the advantages the problems that need to be solved ensures that the argument is complete. Second, demonstrating with the best evidence available that the proposal solves problems is persuasive. Third, ordering and naming advantages according to the order and language of the identified problems can assist the audience with anticipating arguments and render arguments more comprehensible.

The second function of advantages is that they intensify desire. Occupying the minds of the audience with impressions of a remedied world has persuasive power. Alan Monroe's motivated sequence introduces and explains what he terms the "visualization" component of a persuasive appeal. In *Principles of Speech*, Monroe explains that the goal of visualization "is to intensify desire."[4] "Its purpose," according to Monroe, "is to make your listeners really want to see the belief accepted by everyone or to see the proposal adopted and carried out."[5] As the stock issue of solution is the equivalent of Monroe's "satisfaction" step, advantages are the equivalent of Monroe's visualization step. Monroe's emphasis on visualization punctuates the value of the power of advantages to persuade beyond the measured and logical description of a plan's ability to solve a problem. Helping people vividly imagine a solution, like allowing them to test-drive a car, enables the audience to approximate the feel of the new and improved world.

President Obama illustrated this phenomenon in his healthcare address on September 9, 2009, to a joint session of Congress, when he outlined a vision of the future for the American people:

> What this plan will do is make the insurance you have work better for you. Under this plan, it will be against the law for insurance companies to deny you coverage because of a preexisting condition. As soon as I sign this bill, it will be against the law for insurance companies to drop your coverage when you get sick or water it down when you need it the most. They will no longer be able to place some arbitrary cap on the amount of coverage you can receive in a given year or in a lifetime. We will place a limit on how much you can be charged for out-of-pocket expenses, because in the United States of America, no one should go broke because they get sick. And insurance companies will be required to cover, with no extra charge, routine checkups and preventive care, like mammograms and colonoscopies – because there's no reason we shouldn't be catching diseases like breast cancer and colon cancer before they get worse. That makes sense, it saves money, and it saves lives.

In plain language, the tangible and immediate benefits of healthcare reform are laid out for a nation's consideration.

In the next chapter, we begin our consideration of reasoning in public policy advocacy.

Exercise 3: Identifying Stock Issues

Typically, you can only identify stock issues by stepping back from a single advocacy event and surveying the controversy more broadly and perhaps historically. Your task with this exercise is to (a) choose a controversy, (b) determine the proposition under which advocacy is taking place in the controversy, (c) identify the stock issues (i.e., problem, cause, solution, and advantages) associated with at least one problem claimed by an affirmative advocate operating within the controversy, and (d) provide quotations (and citations) from the affirmative advocates – use their words directly, when possible.

Notes

1. For an excellent study of the human costs of war in Iraq, see: Gilbert Burnham, Shannon Doocy, Elizabeth Dzeng, Riyadh Lafta, and Les Roberts, "The Human Cost of the War in Iraq: A Mortality Study, 2002–2006," Bloomberg School of Public Health, December 12, 2012. Accessed September 28, 2013, http://web.mit.edu/CIS/pdf/Human_Cost_of_War.pdf.

2. Lee Hultzen, "Status in Deliberative Analysis," in *The Rhetorical Idiom: Essays in Rhetoric, Oratory, Language, and Drama*, ed. Donald Cross Bryant (Ithaca, NY: Cornell University Press, 1958).

3. See Kathryn M. Olson, "The Practical Importance of Inherency Analysis for Public Advocates: Rhetorical Leadership in Framing a Supportive Social Climate for Education Reforms," *Journal of Applied Communication Research*, 36:2 (2008): 219–241.

4. Alan Monroe, *Principles of Speech* (Glenview, IL: Scott, Foresman, and Company, 1943), 97.

5. Ibid., 97.

· 4 ·

EVALUATING REASONING

Takeaways

1. Evaluating reasoning permits you to uncover the often invisible logic that drives all advocacy. Learning how to discern the assumptions and conclusions upon which advocates base their claims is vital to effective public policy advocacy.
2. There are relatively simple critical questions that may make you more efficient at interrogating the reasons you offer, and those offered by others, in support of policy proposals.
3. The critical questions you pose are the same questions you can assume the target audience will pose, and thus such questions form the tenets of a common rationality.

Introduction

In this chapter, we introduce guiding principles and some critical questions you can use to construct reasonable arguments and evaluate the arguments offered by others. *If you are an affirmative advocate (seeking to change the status quo*), you will construct effective reasons for adopting your proposal. *If you are a negative advocate (seeking to maintain the status quo)*, you will evaluate and refute the reasons offered by someone seeking to change the status quo.

In this chapter, we (1) describe the basic and practical characteristics of arguments that are presented in public policy advocacy and (2) offer an explanation of the most common form of reasoning in public policy advocacy – causal reasoning – and an arrangement of critical questions designed to make you more efficient at interrogating causal reasoning. By introducing the critical questions associated with reasoning, we will also introduce you to some of the most commonly marshaled argument forms used primarily by the negative advocate, including the barrier, the disadvantage, and the turnaround.

The Basics of Reasoning

Reasoning refers to *how advocates link ideas and evidence they believe their audience will accept to conclusions they hope their audience will draw.* Students of argumentation and debate are often taught complex and rigid rules of formal logic to determine whether arguments are well-reasoned, basic principles of causality, deduction, induction, and so forth, and we will explain some of these principles in this and the next chapter. But you will also learn that everyday advocacy rarely involves such a systematic presentation of elements such as major and minor premises; and, one or more key points are typically missing when an advocate expresses his or her position within ordinary, everyday advocacy settings. Thus, evaluating reasoning involves a mental assembly of what is stated and what is not stated.

Let us begin with an example. Consider the following argument one might have encountered in the late 1990s:

> When a president lies to the American people, he should be impeached. Bill Clinton lied to the American people, so he should be impeached.

This example of public policy advocacy was an actual matter before the U.S. House of Representatives (who voted for impeachment on December 19, 1998) and the U.S. Senate (who voted to acquit the president on February 12, 1999). It is not difficult to appreciate that there is a certain grace to this argument. It follows the structure of what logicians would call a "categorical deductive syllogism." One can "deduce" the claim that something or someone belongs to a category from the major and minor "premises." Following the rules of logic, *if* the major premise and minor premise are true, *it follows logically that* the conclusion will be true. As such:

> Major premise: *All Presidents who lie to the American people should be impeached;*
> Minor premise: *Bill Clinton lied to the American people;*
> Conclusion: *Therefore, Bill Clinton should be impeached.*

However, if you follow the advice of philosopher Steven Toulmin, you will seek a simpler means of identifying the components of arguments.[1] Premises, argues Toulmin, can rarely be assessed as "true" or "false," and only advocates in the most formal argument settings speak in a structure closely approximating a syllogism. Toulmin draws attention to how advocates bridge "data" and a "claim" with a "warrant," in his well-known model:

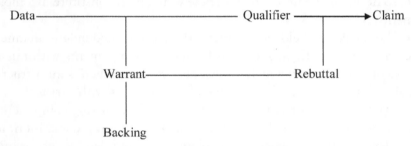

The "claim" is the conclusion the advocate wishes the audience will draw. "Data" is another term for "evidence," but it might also involve more simply an explanation or idea that supports the claim. The "warrant" links the data and the claim and thus serves as a basic term labeling the reasoning strategy of the advocate. Here is the argument for impeachment laid out in Toulmin's model:

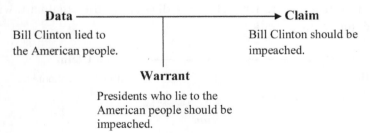

Often a warrant is further bolstered with additional data or information, which Toulmin refers to as "backing." Backing for the above claim might be as simple as the belief that "a president who violates the trust of the American people in one instance cannot be trusted in all future matters." Taken together, the warrant and its backing offer an indication of *how advocates link claims and evidence they believe their audience will accept to conclusions they hope their audiences will draw.* The two additional components Toulmin provides (qualifier and rebuttal) offer additional insights into the potential weaknesses of an argument.[2]

Toulmin's scheme can also illustrate the manner in which certain assumptions that link facts or data to a conclusion are often unstated. What if the impeachment argument did not include what Toulmin labels the warrant? For example, during the proceedings in 1998 that led to the impeachment of President Bill Clinton, we might have heard someone say, "Bill Clinton should be impeached," or the more telling, "Bill Clinton lied to the American people so he should be impeached." These would both constitute incomplete arguments.

In the academic field of argumentation, these incomplete arguments are referred to as "enthymemes." Enthymemes are arguments with missing premises or a situation in which some aspect of an argument's infrastructure is missing. The concept of an enthymeme originates with Aristotle, who wrote about it in his ancient text, *On Rhetoric.*[3] The missing component of the larger argument is filled in by the audience to form a conclusion, and this tendency of the audience to complete the incomplete argument offers an advocate an opportunity to strategically connect to the audience. The missing premise, therefore, is typically an idea advocates can assume will be shared by a large portion of a message's target audience. In the above examples advocating impeachment, the critical assumption, *"Presidents who lie to the American people should be impeached,"* is missing, as well as any subsequent backing that indicates why the maker of this argument believes that *any* lie warrants impeachment. Here is a diagram of the argument, with the missing component in italics:

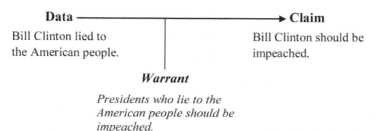

Data ———————————————————▶ **Claim**

Bill Clinton lied to   Bill Clinton should be
the American people.   impeached.

Warrant

*Presidents who lie to the
American people should be
impeached.*

By contending with the unstated assumption, the opposition can consider reasons why some might not believe that *all presidents who lie to the American people should be impeached*. For some, it would depend on the subject of the lie – the national budget, war, or private family matters, for example – or the costs of the lie in terms of national treasure or life – whether anyone was seriously hurt by the lie or died because of the lie, for example. Each of these factors could be presented to challenge the claim and expand the depth and range of the debate. Once you have determined the warrant, you could begin a line of discussion over whether a president is ever justified in lying to the American people. However, if you are opposed to impeachment and limit your rebuttal to countering only what is stated, you may not pose productive objections and the resulting debate might be considerably less rigorous. You might engage in a definitional or philosophical debate over what constitutes a "lie" in order to deal with the fact that Bill Clinton did, indeed, tell the American people something that was not true.[4] An important consequence of countering only what is stated, in this case, is that you might inadvertently agree with the warrant of the proponent of impeachment – that *presidents who lie to the American people should be impeached*. The resulting debate would achieve little in terms of evaluating the specific policy proposal. Instead, as we indicate below, challenging the specific policy proposal, or advocating an alternative course of action, would be more productive.

The impeachment argument illustrates how the evaluation of reasoning requires an engagement with assumptions and implied points. Next, we will consider a policy-centered approach to the evaluation of reasoning, beginning with the most common form of reasoning in public policy advocacy: causal reasoning.

Critical Questions

For us, lessons about reasoning are exhilarating and empowering, but we will not pretend that learning about the forms of reasoning common in public policy advocacy will be super exciting for everyone. Separated from the real-time experience of actual advocacy, these concepts can seem disconnected from anything occurring in your life. In our coaching and teaching of argumentation and debate, we focus on two overarching advantages to learning about reasoning and ask you now to consider them. First, the manner in which advocates *reason* to arrive at their conclusion is the infrastructure, or internal strategy, that holds up a reason for believing something. Without a sound infrastructure, advocates can be criticized for failing to make the case or simply thinking sensibly about a problem. Advocates seek to discover the substance behind a call for reform or defense of the status quo, and that substance is an appeal's essential architecture or its *infrastructure*. If you think of a building that seems to effortlessly stand against opposing forces (gravity, weather, natural and human-made disasters), you know that something behind the façade holds it all together. A common revelation among new students of argument is that unveiling the existence and inadequacies of an argument's infrastructure is often a significant step to casting doubt among an audience considering that argument.

Second, understanding the infrastructure of an argument is especially important in public policy advocacy because so much advocacy in the public sphere is presented in an incomplete manner. We make the point throughout the prior chapter that an argument presented in a particular advocacy situation is almost always only a part of the larger public appeal of advocates or only a small portion of a larger controversy. Similarly, here we note that advocates may offer only a brief concern or complaint and leave it to the audience to fill in the remaining logic. Some advocates are simply outraged. People are being shot near their homes or schools and they want it to stop. Their relatives are being deported and they want it to stop. Their business is being overburdened by taxes and fees and they want it to stop. These dynamics may bring advocates into the public sphere where they will make demands of people in positions of power; but as powerful as outrage is as a driving force for activism, it does not naturally result in a clear articulation of a policy objective. Understanding the infrastructure of an argument helps you form a more complete picture of the larger appeal and its context.

There are many excellent systems for evaluating reasoning that accommodate the practical characteristics of public policy advocacy. As we have noted, our introduction to argumentation and debate was influenced heavily by Robert Huber's "lines of argument" approach, which can now be found in Huber and Snider's text.[5] However, our challenge with this and other systems that offer stock objections has been teaching students to match the particular objections to the particular offenses.[6] With extensive study and practice, such objections can be marshaled with great skill and contribute to effective problem-solving engagements. However, to empower you to enter the realm of public policy advocacy, to give you confidence that you can affect the outcome of an issue without extensive training in debate, we favor an approach that poses a limited set of *critical questions* designed to assist your own critical thinking and discover flaws in the reasoning of others.

The deployment of critical questions is a system of evaluating reasoning – and, in the next chapters, evaluating evidence – that imagines how an advocate's reasoning will be evaluated by his or her target audience. As we explain in more detail in chapter eight, we believe you and your audience can be considered separated from one another only artificially. When it comes to evaluating reasoning, for all practical purposes, you should consider yourself part of the public you address and seek to convince. In so doing, you must also assume – and we believe safely so – that all those who are part of this public audience share with you an affinity for common patterns of thinking or ways of constructing claims that are viewed as rational within a community. You should endeavor to conform to these patterns and ways if you wish to effectively communicate your concerns and convince your audience to accept or reject a policy proposal.[7] In a public policy controversy, affirmative advocates will be the first to evaluate the reasons that make up their policy proposal, followed by their intended audience (the public, decision makers, including those who might oppose the proposal). Therefore, if you are proposing a policy change, you should assume that these critical questions are inevitable responses of your audience even if you have failed to pose them yourself in regard to your own advocacy.

Obviously, it would be more strategically wise of you to evaluate your own reasoning before subjecting your policy proposals to the scrutiny of your target audience. As a practical matter, if any of these critical questions are to become convincing refutation, they must be reformulated into statements refuting the claims of either affirmative or negative advocates. For example, if you are a negative advocate, you will want to know, "Will the proposed solution cause additional problems not already occurring in the status quo?" If your answer is "yes," you might reformulate the question into a statement for the purposes of refutation: "The proposal causes a problem that is not already occurring," or you might move directly to articulating the specific problem caused by the proposal, which would have the same impact ("Building on that land will cause flooding," or "The proposal to go to war will lead to long-term destabilization of the region"). Thus, the critical questions are intended to guide your evaluation of advocacy, not necessarily to be repeated verbatim in the speeches and written material that make up your actual advocacy; however, if you were to simply invert the question to a statement, followed by an explanation, you would at least be engaged in productive refutation.

In the next section, we describe what we consider to be the most common form of reasoning in public policy advocacy: causal reasoning. We offer an arrangement of critical questions intended to make you more efficient at inter-rogating the causal reasons offered by you and others. These critical questions form a macro-level framework of evaluation that calls on you to begin your evaluation of public policy advocacy by attending first to the causal claims being made to support a policy proposal. As you will learn in the next chapter, isolated arguments are supported by a variety of reasoning infrastructures, but we strongly recommend that you begin your analysis by asking whether the policy goal is well-reasoned. *Is the proposal supported by you or another address-ing a problem caused by something in the status quo, and can that problem be solved?* The above impeachment argument is an example of how you might be dis-tracted by the stated argument and fail to address the policy goals. It would be relatively easy for you to address the advocate for impeachment on the basis of what he or she has said and how his or her claim is structured. You would determine that the argument relies on deductive reasoning and that one of the premises is not exactly "true," point out that "it depends on the subject of the lie," and voila, you've won the argument! But, might you have instead assumed that the advocate for impeachment is advocating for a specific policy goal – impeachment – and that goal requires an analysis of the problem, the cause, a clear plan for removing the president and installing a new person, and a thorough consideration of advantages (and disadvantages)? The crit-ical questions below are designed to be your first priority (see **Appendix** for a list of all critical questions recommended for the evaluation of reasoning and evidence). By focusing first on causal reasoning, we focus attention on the central burdens of advocacy in the realm of public policy; however, an appreciation for the mechanics of other forms of reasoning will complete an essential toolkit for critical thinking and problem solving.

Predictions in Public Policy Advocacy: Evaluating Causal Reasoning

Consider this imaginary situation that illustrates the role of causal reasoning. In this case, the setting is an interpersonal one with which you may be famil-iar. Imagine yourself wanting to be supportive of a good friend who just went through a breakup. You arrive at your friend's home and find him or her lying around, with no plans, obviously very depressed, and with little apparent hope for the future. You suggest the two of you go see a movie, a comedy romance that's doing very well at the box office.

You claim: *"It will get your mind off the breakup."*

Your friend replies: *"I'd rather not. Going to see that movie will just depress me."*

You respond: *"There are other movies, of course, but it seems to me you're already depressed, so the movie isn't going to cause that problem. It might actually make you more hopeful about the next chapter of your life."*

Beginning with the thinking that gave rise to the proposal and throughout, both you and your friend are engaged in causal reasoning and challenges related to causal reasoning.

Public policy controversies are essentially two or more sides predicting the future based on cause-effect claims – *if we do* X, Y *will most likely occur*, or more simply, X *will lead to* Y. As noted in chapter one, public policy advocacy is "deliberative" speech, which means it is speech about the *future*. Recognizing that most claims debated in the realm of public policy are predictions focuses attention on the end point, or hypothetical consequences asserted by advocates, and permits advocates on the other side of an issue to counter such claims with significant causal claims of their own.

In the above example involving your invitation to a friend, you make a proposal based on a prediction that seeing a movie may *cause* your friend to feel better (thus you take the affirmative side). Your friend doubts your prediction and counters with an alleged potential disadvantage: that a movie may *cause* him or her to become depressed (thus taking the negative side). The exchange continues with asking critical questions about your friend's causal reasoning, leading to your response that any depression in the aftermath of the movie could not be blamed on the movie on the grounds that he or she is *already* depressed, as the major cause of that depression is the breakup. Indeed, you claim that the movie may actually produce an advantage: to *cause* your friend to be more hopeful about their future.

In our experience, newcomers to the activity of advocacy are quite capable of objecting to faulty causal reasoning. This is perhaps due to the manner in which humans learn through causal reasoning: *If I do* X, *I will be fed. If I avoid* Y, *I will be safe.* There are scores of real-life examples of young children, well before they learn very much at all in formal education settings, running from danger or taking action they believe will lead to a desirable outcome. As you grow into adulthood and begin to apply your causal reasoning skills to problems you encounter or proposals put to you by others, you learn what it means to reason wisely. Particularly as it pertains to the development of solutions to problems, you learn it is especially important to focus on causal reasoning. Consider again the stock issues discussed in chapter three – problem, cause, solution, advantages. The connection between the problem and the cause involves a causal claim that the mechanics of an insufficient status quo – the cause – is producing harms – the problem. Likewise, the link between the solution and the advantages relies on causal reasoning, a claim that a policy proposal will lead to the removal or significant reduction of a problem. This basic structure is part of the anatomy of everyday public discourse. Causal relationships are almost always speculative, and claiming that X *causes* Y or X *will likely lead to* Y carries inevitable risks. Even in the realm of science, where "factual" determinations of cause and effect are regular tasks, accepted explanations and settled questions are merely agreed-upon explanations that have yet to be disproved. Well-known examples of controversies over causal reasoning include whether human activity causes global warming and whether global warming constitutes a long-term or permanent threat to humans and other life on earth, whether violent video games cause young users to become violent themselves, whether marijuana use leads to more dangerous substance abuse, whether immigration reform will lead to an increase in illegal immigration or loss of jobs for legal residents, whether the death penalty deters individuals from murdering others, and the list goes on. In each case, academically credentialed and articulate authorities, committed to their causal claims, must contend with challenges from other credentialed and articulate authorities offering other causal explanations.

There are some relatively basic critical questions that can permit you to exercise more control over the causal claims made within public policy controversies. Those evaluating the causal reasoning of a policy proposal should ask (and, in the case of the audience, *will likely ask*) the following six critical questions:

1. Is the identified cause significant enough to produce the problem?
2. Are there other probable causes that might reasonably produce the problem?
3. Will the proposed solution solve the problem?
4. Is there something about the status quo that will prevent the proposed solution from working?
5. Will the proposed solution cause additional problems or disadvantages not already occurring in the status quo?
6. Is an identified disadvantage the likely result of the proposed solution, or might it be caused by other factors?

The above six questions deal directly with the stock issues discussed in chapter three and, as such, represent the most common concerns of those wishing to construct a compelling affirmative position or inclined to defend the status quo. Once these questions have been asked and answered to some degree, they also become components of a framework of refutation. As noted above, if any of these critical questions are to become convincing refutation, the answers should inform the statements used to advocate for, or to refute, claims.

Consider this framework applied to an example of a policy proposal. Imagine you are an activist concerned with the spread of HIV/AIDs in a particular region or nation of Africa. You argue the problem is caused by the failure of that region's government to promote the use of condoms and call on the U.S. federal government to provide more funding of condom distribution efforts. If you are proposing this policy, you should imagine that the audience, including advocates opposing your solution, will pose the critical questions above. The *first critical question* concerns the cause of the problem. Those opposed to your solution argue that the regional government's failure to promote condom use (what you allege is the cause) may explain only a small portion of the problem or may not be a reasonable explanation at all. The opposition may provide evidence that the regional government is already involved in an extensive and progressive condom promotion effort, which leads to the *second critical question* concerning other probable causes of the spread of HIV/AIDs in the region, which, the opposition argues, includes a cultural aversion among males in the region to use condoms and an unwillingness of male leaders to address this widespread reluctance. Concerning the *third critical question*, you are fairly confident that the U.S. federal government has the capacity to fund (their actions would lead to, or *cause*) a large-scale condom distribution effort in the target region; however, the opposition provides evidence to indicate that increased funding by the United States has led to no appreciable decrease in the spread of HIV/AIDs in the region. There's a reason for this, argues the opposition, raising the *fourth critical question*, and this concerns a particular dynamic of a civil conflict in the region: a propaganda campaign by one of the leading factions that is convincing men and women that contraceptives provided by foreign governments are unsafe and potentially damaging to users. While misguided and inaccurate, this information will prevent sexually active individuals in the region from using the condoms provided by your plan. You argue that a U.S.-sponsored intervention may work to change the thinking of the people of the region, but the negative poses the *fifth critical question* and argues there is a significant disadvantage to providing more funds to the government of this region. Evidence indicates this government has been channeling donated funds intended to reduce the spread of HIV/AIDs to weapons purchases that are fueling a burgeoning civil war. Experts claim any additional weapons added to the conflict will exacerbate the situation, leading to a fear among the population of genocide, resulting widespread famine, and a refugee crisis. Finally, concerning the *sixth critical question*, you argue that the civil conflict was well under way before your proposal and, therefore, the policy you have proposed could not be said to uniquely cause the disadvantage.

This hypothetical example illustrates the manner in which the six critical questions can pose major challenges to the causal infrastructure of a proposal. If you are an affirmative advocate, your primary reason for believing that your proposal is warranted requires a series of believable causal claims, which negative advocates will challenge. Knowing you will face a challenge, you have an initial opportunity to pose these critical questions yourself, anticipating the concerns of negative advocates and preparing for them. Likewise, if you find yourself in the role of negative advocate, these six critical questions should serve as a starting point for your evaluation of the causal claims of the affirmative advocate. By asking these questions, you will uncover flaws in the causal reasoning that undergirds a policy proposal.

While the first three questions recall the stock issues and represent essential burdens of affirmative advocates and basic requirements of causal reasoning in the realm of problem solving, the second three form a framework for negative advocacy that requires more explanation. The fourth question concerns whether there is something about the status quo that will prevent a proposed solution from working. The answer to that question can lead you to discover what are sometimes referred to as "counteracting causes" or "barriers" that will prevent the solution from working. Counteracting causes and barriers are realities of the status quo that, a negative advocate alleges, the policy proposal does not seek to or cannot change, which will continue to cause the problem; or they may be aspects of the status quo or the proposal that will interrupt the effectiveness of the proposal. The claim that barriers or counteracting causes will prevent the achievement of an advantage is a significant tool for negative advocates, which allows the negative to argue that some aspect of the status quo or proposal will prevent the advantages from taking hold. Properly supported, such arguments can be devastating to the causal reasoning undergirding affirmative advocacy. The identification of a barrier is not a line of argument used exclusively by negative advocates; affirmative advocates can respond similarly to a disadvantage claimed by a negative advocate, in which the affirmative advocate claims that some aspect or outcome of the policy offered will counteract the alleged negative consequence of the advantage. A counteracting cause may also be introduced by an affirmative advocate to claim that the causal relationship that allegedly produces the disadvantage (that a plan will cause a disadvantage) will be interrupted by some counteracting force of the status quo.

A policy proposal may also be criticized for not being appropriately structured to deal with the problem. That is, the proposal itself may be a barrier due to, for example, its inadequate funding or limited time frame. When the Obama administration, through executive order, implemented a policy of "deferred action for childhood arrivals," or "DACA," many young people who were brought to the United States illegally by their parents were provided an opportunity to register their presence in the United States and receive a form of legal status and worker authorization. Many immigration reform advocates, while pleased with the shift in policy, noted that the age limitation – those who were under the age of 31 as of June 15, 2012 – made it impossible for many equally innocent childhood arrivals to receive the same protection against the harsh and irreversible consequences of deportation or the inability to legally work in the United States. Would not the same logic that applied to a 29-year-old apply to a 31-year-old? A 31-year-old "dreamer" might reasonably argue that the policy causes him or her to be treated as a criminal when, prior to the policy, he or she was viewed by many to be as innocent as his or her younger peers.[8]

The fifth and sixth critical questions concerning causal reasoning deal with potential "disadvantages." The fifth critical question – *Will the proposed solution cause additional problems or disadvantages not already occurring in the status quo?* – is a standard question raised by the audience of a public policy proposal, although audience members might ask the question in a variety of alternative ways (e.g., "Will there be unintended consequences?" is a common form of this question). Disadvantages are asserted by a negative advocate in defense of the status quo. They are causal claims—*policy X will cause disadvantage Y*, argues the negative. Most disadvantages assume that the proposal will be enacted and ask *what will occur after enactment*. Consider the following example: On February 12, 2003, U.S. Senator Robert C. Byrd sought to convince his colleagues that preemptive war with Iraq could have devastating and irreversible consequences for the people of Iraq, America, and the world. Byrd argued that "we hear little about the *aftermath* of war in Iraq" [italics added], setting up the opportunity to outline what some of the consequences might be, beginning with the failure to complete the mission in Afghanistan. "In the absence of plans, speculation abroad is rife," he contemplated:

> Will we seize Iraq's oil fields, becoming an occupying power which controls the price and supply of that nation's oil for the foreseeable future? To whom do we propose to hand the reigns of power after Saddam Hussein? Will our war inflame the Muslim world, resulting in devastating attacks on Israel? Will Israel retaliate with its own nuclear arsenal? Will the Jordanian and Saudi Arabian governments be toppled by radicals bolstered by Iran, which has much closer ties to terrorism than Iraq? Could the disruption of the world's oil supply lead to a worldwide recession? Has our senselessly bellicose language and our callous disregard of the interests and opinions of other nations increased the global race to join the nuclear club and made proliferation an even more lucrative practice for nations which need the income?[9]

The questions posed by Byrd have one overriding common quality: if inverted from a question to a claim, each is a hypothetical disadvantage he believed then was probable. Each of these are predictions that rely on causal reasoning that should be evaluated.

Disadvantages are structured in a wide variety of ways. In practical political discourse, such as Byrd's concerns above, disadvantages may be expressed simply as "negative impacts" or "unintended consequences" of a policy. Ideally, negative advocates alleging a disadvantage will:

(1) Identify something about the policy proposal that will cause an undesirable effect.
(2) Claim that the effect is significant.

Before these essential components are provided, disadvantages are typically "named" in some way; ideally, this will be a full sentence claim, such as: "Preemptive war with Iraq will have devastating and irreversible consequences for the people of Iraq, America, and the world." Or, advocates will name their disadvantages in a manner that highlights the consequences specifically: "Worldwide recession will occur if we go to war with Iraq."

If one or more disadvantages are offered by a negative advocate, the sixth question will place the same reasoning burdens of the affirmative on the negative advocate. By asking, *Is an identified disadvantage the likely result of the proposed solution, or might it be caused by other factors?* the affirmative advocate begins a process of uncovering a wide range of potential flaws in the reasoning infrastructure on which a disadvantage relies. This begins with questioning whether the negative advocate has identified a particular aspect of the affirmative policy proposal that will cause the consequences. The affirmative advocate is essentially turning the causal challenges that may have been posed against his or her advocacy against the negative advocate's causal claims, beginning with the first critical question: *Is the identified cause [in this case, the affirmative policy proposal] significant enough to produce the problem [the disadvantage]?* If the affirmative advocate's answer is no, which it is likely to be, he or she will argue that the negative advocate failed to prove that the policy proposal contains any specific element that will cause the disadvantage.

The battle over whether an appropriate link between the affirmative proposal and the consequences of the disadvantage has been established is often complicated by a claimed chain of events that allegedly leads to an unreasonable end point. In defending a proposal against a severe negative consequence that lies at the end of a complex chain of events, it is often sufficient to demonstrate that a chain of causation is not sufficiently backed by evidence. For negative advocates, it is generally acceptable, and perhaps wise, not to go too far along the causal chain (nuclear devastation, for example) unless there is very strong evidence to support the dire outcomes being predicted. Offering generally undesirable impacts (regional conflict, economic recession, drought, and so forth) and permitting the audience to contemplate where such impacts could lead is often sufficient.

The second critical question – *Are there other probable causes which might reasonably produce the problem?* – can also be asked by the affirmative advocate in an effort to discover that another cause within the status quo is *already* producing a claimed disadvantage. The logical conclusion, argues the affirmative advocate, is that his or her policy proposal cannot be said to be the only or even a significant cause of the disadvantage. For example, opponents of U.S. intervention in the Syrian civil war might argue that arming the anti-governmental forces would empower anti-American extremists fighting alongside the rebels, permitting additional hostilities in neighboring Iraq. In response, proponents of U.S. intervention might argue (and provide evidence to prove) that anti-American extremists are *already* fighting alongside the rebels, are *already* amply armed, and are *already* engaged in hostilities in neighboring Iraq. There are two common defenses negative advocates offer in favor of the causal claims that make up their disadvantages. The first is to simply argue that, even if the status quo is already experiencing the problem, that problem is made worse by a policy proposal. The second is to be more precise about the timing of the alleged disadvantage, arguing that the consequences are close at hand and the affirmative proposal will produce the conditions that cause them to occur.

Another argument form that is a common causal argument in public policy advocacy is referred to as a "turn." When a negative advocate claims that *the proposed solution will cause disadvantages*, affirmative advocates can "turn" the analysis around, claiming that the logical effect of a disadvantage may, in some way, *just as likely* be helpful to the values and desires of the affirmative. Turns are highly effective arguments because – theoretically – they take over an entire portion of the negative advocate's advocacy and transform it into a new advantage in favor of the affirmative (the disadvantage, thus, becomes an advantage). If a city council (affirmative advocate) is considering the adoption of an ordinance that would pay all construction workers performing publically funded work the area-standard wage – what is sometimes called the "prevailing wage" – an opponent of the ordinance (negative advocate) might argue that the adoption of a uniform prevailing wage law will cause many low-income, primarily minority workers to lose their jobs (a disadvantage). This is because, alleges the negative advocate, underprivileged workers tend to be employed by smaller construction contractors who do not have the cash flow to pay such high wages before getting paid by the city for the project, and these contractors will lose work that is presently being awarded to them because they perform the work more cheaply, and jobs for underprivileged workers, as a result, will be lost. This presents affirmative advocates an opportunity to argue that the proposed law *will just as likely* promote improved opportunity for these low-income workers and prevent exploitation of underprivileged workers who are currently receiving substandard wages. The ability of the proposed law to positively impact underprivileged workers, claims the affirmative advocate, constitutes another advantage – in effect, that his or her plan leads to better opportunities for underprivileged, primarily minority, job seekers. Thus, the disadvantage is turned into an advantage.

In the next chapter, we continue our discussion of reasoning by considering three additional forms of reasoning and associated critical questions.

Exercise 4: Using Knowledge of Reasoning in a Critique of a Newspaper Opinion Piece (I)

Select a letter to the editor, column, or editorial wherein the writer is addressing a public controversy. Identify the controversy and which side of the issue the writer is on, if possible. Determine the "cause" of the problem the writer is addressing, as he or she might define it. Then ask and answer the first and second critical question for causal reasoning (see above or Appendix).

Notes

1. Stephen Toulmin, *The Uses of Argument*, rev. ed. (Cambridge: Cambridge University Press, 2003).
2. Toulmin's "qualifier" consists of any clear indication of the level of commitment an advocate has to his or her claim (indicated through the use of terms such as "probably," "likely," "certainly," "absolutely," etc.). The "rebuttal" imagines a counter position. The rebuttal acts as a counter to the warrant and is best imagined as a statement beginning with the term "unless." The rebuttal might also serve to counter the data (unless the evidence is flawed).
3. Aristotle, *On Rhetoric: A Theory on Civic Discourse*, trans. George Kennedy (Oxford: Oxford University Press, 2006).
4. The lie that was at the center of the case for impeachment was to deny that he had had an extramarital affair with a White House intern. Clinton famously denied the affair in remarks to the media and then later admitted he lied in sworn testimony.
5. Robert B. Huber and Alfred C. Snider, *Influencing through Argument* (Updated Edition) (New York: International Debate Education Association, 2006).
6. Consider the following lines of argument to validate or invalidate causal reasoning from Huber and Snider, 139–145:
   1. The alleged cause lacks the means, power, facilities, and/or desire to produce the suggested effect.
   2. This cannot be the sole cause because of the operation of the following specific causes.
   3. The alleged cause is quite insignificant.
   4. The speaker is ignoring the original cause; at best she is only speaking of a contributing cause.
   5. The following counteracting causes have been or will be operating.
   6. The gentleperson has mistaken coincidence for causal relationship.

   For today's practitioner of public policy advocacy, matching the specific objection to the offense can be especially challenging in the real time of advocacy situations.
7. This conception of the audience as a rational community is at the heart of Chaim Perelman and Lucy Olbrechts-Tyteca's notion of "universal audience," an audience that is imagined by the advocate for practical purposes, an assumed larger society, of which the

advocate is a part, that could be convinced "that the reasons adduced are of a compelling character, that they are self-evident, and possess an absolute and timeless validity, independent of local or historical contingencies" (Chaim Perelman and Lucy Olbrechts-Tyteca, *The New Rhetoric: A Treatise on Argumentation*, John Wilkinson and Purcell Weaver, Trans. (London: University of Notre Dame Press, 1969), 32).

8. On November 20, 2014, based on executive orders issued by President Barack Obama, the U.S. Department of Homeland Security expanded the deferred action provisions and issued guidance that indicated this "age cap" no longer applies to those seeking deferred action (see: U.S. Department of Homeland Security, *Exercising Prosecutorial Discretion with Respect to Individuals Who Came to the United States as Children and with Respect to Certain Individuals Who Are the Parents of U.S. Citizens or Permanent Residents*, by Jeh Charles Johnson, Secretary, November 20, 2014, 3, http://www.dhs.gov/sites/default/files/publications/14_1120_memo_deferred_action.pdf).

9. Robert C. Byrd, *Losing America: Confronting a Reckless and Arrogant Presidency* (New York: W. W. Norton & Company, 2005), 247–248.

· 5 ·

REASONING BY OTHER MEANS

Takeaways

1. Evaluating these additional forms of reasoning is often necessary for understanding the nuances of thought behind causal claims and predictions.
2. When dealing with a deductive or inductive claim or an analogy, your first line of strategy should be to isolate the recommended policy or conclusion and debate it on its merits – whether the policy solves a problem without causing other new problems that are more troubling than the original problem.

Introduction

The critical questions associated with causal reasoning are the most effective means of interrogating the proposals offered by public policy advocates, but the logic of advocates can also be profitably subjected to objections associated with other forms of reasoning considered in this chapter: reasoning by deduction, induction, and analogy. This chapter examines these other forms of reasoning in order.

In public policy advocacy, rarely does a purely deductive or inductive argument or an argument based on an analogy exist outside of a larger policy claim that relies primarily on a causal infrastructure. A simpler way to make this point is to note that a causal claim – that something leads to or will lead to something else – are typically supported by an infrastructure of claims that include deductive, inductive, or analogically derived claims. While you may stumble upon a deductive or inductive claim or an analogy in the midst of a policy controversy, *your first line of strategy should be to isolate the recommended policy or conclusion and debate it on its merits*, which will likely take you squarely to the critical questions associated with causal reasoning. This point was made in the prior chapter concerning the deductive argument calling for the impeachment of Bill Clinton. Just because impeachment can be logically deduced from a major and minor premise, this does not make the policy goal of impeachment an ideal solution to a problem. You are altogether better off asking the six critical questions pertaining to causal reasoning *first* to determine what advantages are being claimed by the advocates for the policy proposal and what disadvantages may result from the policy proposal before evaluating the micro-level reasoning underwriting a policy proposal. The flaws to which deductive or inductive arguments or claims supported by analogies might be susceptible, then, should prompt, but not stand in for, policy debate.

Reasoning by Deduction

Deductive reasoning is reasoning in its most classical or traditional sense. In this section, we provide some basic lessons that will assist you in recognizing the flaws of your own deductive reasoning and the reasoning of others in the realm of public policy advocacy. You will recall from the impeachment example that the conclusion was deduced as a logical outcome of the premises. In most argumentation and debate textbooks, the term "syllogism" is usually used to describe two premises (a "major" and "minor"), followed by a conclusion. A syllogism deduces knowledge about a specific instance from acceptance of a general principle. A classic example of a syllogism is the following:

Major Premise: *All humans are mortal.*
Minor Premise: *Lucy is a human.*
Conclusion: *Therefore, Lucy is mortal.*

This syllogism has three important terms – A ("humans"), B ("mortal"), and C ("Lucy") – and the validity of a conclusion is dependent on these terms remaining relatively stable in placement and meaning throughout the presentation of the argument, leading to the following mathematically sound formula:

$$All\ A = B$$
$$C = A$$
$$Therefore\ C = B$$

Once you are introduced to these components of a syllogism, you may also learn that there are a range of offenses an advocate can commit by not keeping each significant term in its correct place or if the meaning of one of the terms changes between its first and subsequent uses. While these standards, if committed to memory, will assist you in evaluating reasoning, they are less likely to provide particular objections that will register clearly with your target audience in the realm of public policy advocacy.

A deductive structure may serve as a common vehicle for a public policy proposal (the argument for impeachment, for example), but you should ask first whether the policy is one that solves a problem without causing other new problems that are more troubling than the original problem. Beginning with the six critical questions pertaining to causal reasoning, you should *first* determine what advantages are being claimed by advocates for the policy proposal and what disadvantages may result from the policy, as your ability to convince an audience to, or not to, support the policy will be based – over and above other considerations – on whether the policy offers an outcome that is better than the status quo. Once you consider the policy objectives in this manner, the critical questions we offer for the evaluation of deductive reasoning will assist your effort to reveal key assumptions and flaws in reasoning that will give you a clearer picture of what an advocate is attempting to accomplish.

Two main types of arguments rely on deductive reasoning and are especially common in public policy advocacy: *categorical* and *disjunctive*.

Categorical Deduction

The first type of deductive reasoning is *categorical deduction*, which introduces a general conclusion about a set or category of something and then makes a claim about a specific case that arguably fits into that category. The conclusion drawn about the category should apply also to the specific case. It begins with a general rule and follows with a specific case, deducing a conclusion. Essential to the persuasiveness of a categorical argument is the initial claim or major premise, which presents the audience with a general rule. Advocates deploying categorical reasoning count on their audience to accept the general rule and apply the same general characteristics to a specific case.

The history of American public policy is rife with examples of categorical reasoning undergirding some of the most controversial public debates. An example used by Martha Cooper is the claim that "abortion should be illegal." The claim relies on the classification of abortion as murder facilitated by the application of the general rule – murder should be illegal – to abortion (the specific case), as illustrated below:

Murder should be illegal. (general rule)
Abortion is murder. (specific case)
Therefore, abortion should be illegal.

Once the audience learns that an advocate plans to exploit the audience's allegiance to the general rule – to cause them to deduce that the act of abortion (the specific case) should be illegal – those who disagree with the conclusion will focus on whether abortion reasonably belongs to the category or class of human behavior called "murder."

In the realm of public policy, an activity's categorical consistency with another activity is not *per se* a good reason to support the conclusion that naturally follows. In response to the above categorical argument, questions such as *Should the American legal system conclude that abortion is murder?* or *What would be the consequences of classifying abortion as murder?* would address the claims as matters of public policy. That is not to say there is no benefit in identifying the flaws to which categorical reasoning is susceptible. In additional to interrogating the evidence used by the advocate to establish his or her claims, the following critical questions associated with categorical reasoning will assist you in this endeavor:

1. Does the specific case or instance under consideration belong to the general category or rule?
2. Is the specific case or instance under consideration accurate?
3. Are the terms used throughout the argument consistent?

The first two critical questions focus your attention on the action, behavior, occurrence, and so forth, that the advocate believes should be treated in the same manner as the general category or rule. *Can abortion be said to be murder? Is Bill Clinton a president who lied to the American people?* If you believe the answer to either of these questions is no, then presumably you have a reason for believing the specific case does not *belong* to the general category or rule.

The third critical question for categorical arguments concerns the terms used to describe the actions, behaviors, occurrences, and so forth, throughout the description of the general rule, specific case, and conclusion. A flaw occurs when a term shifts in meaning from its original use to something different later in the argument. This is often referred to as "equivocation" – the tendency to rely on the ambiguous nature of certain terms to avoid commitment to a position or to assemble a justification that "sounds" sensible. In the abortion example used to illustrate a categorical argument, the terms are consistently used; that is, they have agreed-upon or at least uniformly understood meanings that are maintained throughout the articulation of the argument. The central dispute will be over whether abortion should be classified as murder and the complexities associated with that controversy. But not all deductive arguments utilize consistent terminology. Anthony Weston, in his review of common fallacies in argument, cites the following particularly complex example of a moment of equivocation:

> Women and men are physically and emotionally different. The sexes are not "equal," then, and therefore the law should not pretend that we are.[1]

Weston makes clear that "[b]etween premise and the conclusion this argument shifts the meaning of the term 'equal,'" where it initially means "identical" to its latter, inferred meaning, where the intended meaning is what women might expect to be entitled to under the law (the same rights and responsibilities as men).[2] Equivocation is tricky business and can take many forms. In the above example, the term "equal" was mentioned only once; its second meaning was implied in a reference to "the law."

Disjunctive Deduction

A second type of deductive reasoning is called *disjunctive deduction*. "Disjunctive" means expressing a choice between mutually exclusive possibilities. "Mutually exclusive" means you cannot do both at the same time. The concept could refer to ideas or beliefs that do not work together, or policy options that cannot be pursued at the same time, because it would be impossible – for example, voting for both the Democratic and the Republican presidential candidate or hiring two people for one job. The concept may also be used to identify a nonsensical choice, one in which one option would produce negative effects that would counteract the positive effects of another option. Advocates deploying disjunctive reasoning offer alternatives and systematically reject the alternatives that do not make sense. Here is an example of a disjunctive argument in the form of a syllogism:

> *The City Council can hire either the Jones firm or Stevenson firm as its architect.*
> *We cannot hire Jones.*
> *Therefore, we must hire Stevenson.*

The terms "either" and "or" signal a disjunctive argument, but the choices may not always be presented in such obvious ways.

We find that disjunctive argument in public policy advocacy can be some of the trickiest argumentation with which to contend. Here is an example of a disjunctive argument that you might encounter at the meeting of any college or university board of trustees:

> *The members of the board have long dealt with the challenges associated with finding the resources to invest in some of our strategic technological initiatives. No one wishes to lessen the quality of our student body by lowering our admissions standards to increase enrollment, but this would increase our revenue. And, we must keep our tuition affordable if we are to remain a viable option for new and existing students, even though increasing tuition would increase our revenue. There is real merit to the idea of adding a fee for courses that involve technology, however.*

These remarks have no "either/or" moments and you do not learn what the advocate favors until the end. It is only after you receive the entire message that you discern the advocate's intent to argue in favor of a new technology fee. Here is how the above argument might be presented as a disjunctive syllogism:

> *In order to raise funds needed to improve technology, we can either lower our admission standards to increase our revenue (A), raise tuition (B), or charge a new fee for courses that involve technology (C).*
> *We cannot lower our admission standards (A) or raise tuition (B).*
> *Therefore, we must charge a new technology fee for courses that involve technology (C).*

More simplistically, this argument can be presented as follows:

> *Either A, B, or C.*
> *Not A or B.*
> *Therefore C.*

In our experience, disjunctive arguments are especially common in professional settings, when leaders introduce several possible solutions to a problem. The disjunctive message structure follows closely the generally agreed-upon process of problem solving that calls for the systematic consideration and review of multiple recommendations. However, similar to the concern expressed above about categorical reasoning, the inadequacy of other options is not *per se* a good reason to support a recommended policy. Before considering the common flaws of disjunctive reasoning, our recommendation would be to isolate the recommended policy and debate whether or not it solves the problem. In the above example, the policy proposal will likely address the immediate need for funds; however, certainly there are some who would argue that increasing costs to students might have a negative impact on enrollment and other major sources of operating revenue for a university (disadvantages). The policy debate would continue along these lines, as it should.

Once you have subjected the favored policy proposal at the end of a disjunctive argument to debate, you may find it useful to assert the common flaws of disjunctive reasoning. These flaws can be discovered by asking the following critical questions:

1. Is the advocate considering all reasonable options?
2. Is the advocate offering good reasons for rejecting options?
3. Are combinations of considered options or other options more reasonable?

In terms of the first critical question, advocates who use disjunctive reasoning often fail to include all reasonably available options. The credibility of the advocate can be a major factor in the acceptance of A, B, or C as the only options; regardless, reasonable options may not actually be limited to either A, B, or C; there may be a D and an E. In the above example, there are relatively obvious alternatives a university board of trustees can take to fund their technology needs, such as efforts to improve the efficiency of information technology resources. These options were not considered by the advocate for change and therefore would have to be evaluated before concluding that the favored option is best.

Other reasonable options are sometimes referred to as "counterplans." Counterplans are typically offered by negative advocates. They are not prompted exclusively by disjunctive reasoning and may appear as a common feature in any public policy controversy. Often negative advocates introduce counterplans simply to stop the momentum of a policy proposal – to "kill the bill," to use a phrase common in legislative settings. If you favor a particular policy proposal and those opposed to your proposal argue that you have not sufficiently considered alternatives, your task is to subject any counterplans to the same critical questions posed in response to any affirmative policy proposal. Thus, the affirmative/negative burdens are reversed for a period of time, as you contend with the alternative option. In general, however, counterplans are rarely presented as full considerations of the problem, as they rely on the work of the affirmative advocate. That is, the negative advocate can often simply offer an alternative plan, since the affirmative advocate already made the fuller case for the need for such a plan.

Your advancement of an alternative option or counterplan in response to a disjunctive argument would require a clear explanation of the counterplan and a demonstration that the counterplan solves the problem *better* than the policy proposal offered at the conclusion of a disjunctive sequence. By "better" we mean to point out that audiences will generally expect that a counterplan will *both* offer advantages that would be lost if the counterplan is not adopted *and* avoid disadvantages associated with the policy proposal favored by the affirmative advocate. In the realm of public policy advocacy, the term "opportunity losses" is sometimes used to describe the benefits lost when an alternative is not pursued (If C is pursued, what will be lost by not choosing A, B, D, or E?).

In terms of the second critical question, another common error in disjunctive reasoning occurs when advocates determine certain options cannot be pursued. The advocate may not have a sensible reason to reject an option. The dismissal of policy options should be justified in accordance with the stock issues we have discussed in chapter three and principles of sound reasoning encouraged by the six critical questions associated with causal reasoning, with the most obvious being, *Will the proposed solution solve the problem?* Consider how the additional critical questions for causal reasoning might be marshaled to determine if options have been properly evaluated.

The third critical question raises the issue of whether an alternative option might be salvaged if it is combined in some productive way with the option favored by the advocate relying on disjunctive reasoning. Just as the advocate may not have a sensible reason to reject an option, he or she may not have a good reason to reject options that could be pursued *with* his or her favored option. The assumption of "mutual exclusivity" – the idea that A cannot be combined with B, C, or D – often drives the dismissal of options that combine policies. A *and* B might be pursued simultaneously to achieve the desired advantage or an alternative advantage that is desired by more stakeholders. The adjoining of two policy options is often referred to as a "permutation." Permutations are essentially a call for "both" – or multiple – plans in some arrangement that addresses potential disadvantages of one or another plan in isolation.

Reasoning by Induction

Reasoning by induction is reasoning by example or examples. A conclusion is drawn through reference to factual occurrences, which can range from a single anecdote to a large collection of statistical data, which, to the satisfaction of advocates citing the example(s), proves the conclusion true. In most cases, advocates will cite more than one example to establish the validity of a claim. This is done because the greater the instances of something occurring, the greater the reliability that, given similar circumstances, something will occur again. In public policy advocacy, examples function as data or evidence, and they rely on what Huber and Snider refer to as "an inductive leap," the assumption that "what is true for the sample will be true for all cases."[3] The conclusion of experts that cigarette smoking causes cancer is inductively derived from numerous studies that show higher incidents of cancer when the studied subjects smoked. Thousands of cases have been studied, and the evidence is so reliable that health officials and other authorities predict outcomes based on the data with regularity.

Inductive reasoning figures prominently in public policy advocacy. You will find it initially to be a means of establishing the existence of a problem. Imagine you support a challenger against an incumbent mayor of your city, and one of the main advantages you claim will result from the challenger's election is "greater openness regarding who the city approves to perform commercial and residential construction development and publically funded construction projects." Part of your complaint, specifically, is that under the incumbent mayor, the planning and procurement processes have largely been conducted in brief meetings where it appears all deliberation and decision making occurred before the meetings. How will you establish this claim? To establish the problem, one option is to cite several examples of high-dollar construction procurement decisions by the city council that involved very little discussion. Such an illustration would rely on reasoning by induction. Affirmative advocates will rely on inductive reasoning to establish the significance of the problem. This is common in claims of injustice, when several instances of individuals being treated unfairly are typically necessary before a community will act to stop the unfair treatment. For example, one or two victims of torture by a foreign government's agents might not be enough to warrant military intervention to overthrow the regime; however, mass torture and genocide – sufficiently proven to have occurred – may justify a policy of intervention. Inductive argument is also used to establish the likelihood that an advantage will occur as a result of a policy proposal, because pointing to another instance of the successful implementation of a solution is a favored means of proving that a policy proposal will be effective. Likewise, negative advocates will cite instances of failure to refute the solvency of a policy proposal.

Considering inductive argument generally, it is difficult to isolate the types of objections inductive reasoning will generate. Cited examples may exist in the form of testimony, studies, surveys, experiments, polls, and other forms of information that are subject to the tests of evidence appropriate for each respective type of evidence. In the above example, the incumbent mayor might have a relatively easy time refuting your inductive argument. He or she might introduce a basic standard regarding what constitutes a "legitimate decision," such as that all decisions were made at meetings open to the public. The mayor may cite several instances of "significant deliberation" and perhaps instances when deliberation led to the rejection of a project. Thus, the mayor may respond with inductive arguments of his or her own. In response, you might select more examples that support your claims, such as decisions in which there was no discussion or questions by the planning commissioners or city council members preceding a vote. And you may isolate a time period of 12 months. The resulting inductive argument might point to a pattern of poor or non-existent public deliberation on matters of consequence to a community.

Similar to our recommendation to focus on the merits of the policy proposal itself in the case of categorical and disjunctive reasoning, when presented with an inductive argument, we recommend that you isolate the policy proposal and pose the critical questions concerning causal reasoning as a first step. Once you have identified the particular claims that are supported or supportable through inductive reasoning, you can pose the following critical questions:

1. Are the instances cited real occurrences as far as can be determined through reliable evidence?
2. Are the instances representative of the practices, behaviors, activities, or phenomena under consideration?
3. Is a single or limited occurrence compelling enough to indicate a problem?

In terms of the first critical question, cited instances are best if they *actually* occurred, because it is too easy for an advocate to construct an ideal set of hypothetical examples that seem realistic. The demand that instances cited be real occurrences is common within debates over proposed anti-discrimination laws, for example. Observing what they consider to be better human relations in other communities, advocates seek to put in place the same or similar anti-discrimination laws adopted by such communities in their own cities. Particularly if the additional protections are likely to impact few or address activity that is unlikely to occur often enough to warrant a change in the law, municipal leaders often ask for real examples of discrimination against residents that involve the specific activity addressed by the proposed amendments. Absent such real examples, leaders are likely to argue that there is no real problem to be addressed.

The second critical question concerns *quality* rather than *quantity*. In the above example concerning amendments proposed to a community's anti-discrimination provisions, the audience might ask, *Are the instances representative of the phenomenon? Are they characteristic of the practices, behaviors, activities, or phenomena advocates seek to address with their proposal?* Instances of violence against transgender individuals might be cited to establish the need for human rights protections, for example. In response, a municipal leader might argue that the instances cited are representative of situations when law enforcement failed to protect individuals against violent criminals but not instances when a transgender individual was unable to receive relief due to a lack of the type of anti-discrimination legislation under consideration.

In terms of the third critical question, it seems wise to accept that there are plenty of instances of single examples being used to draw generalizations that achieve widespread adherence among a public. If one example was a high-profile occurrence that aligned with general views already in place, it may be sufficient to prove a point. In 2003, then Chicago Mayor Richard M. Daley ordered the city's crews to bulldoze Meigs Field, a single strip airport built on a human-made peninsula just east of Soldier Field in downtown Chicago. The demolition, which took place in the middle of the night, was immediately and widely criticized as a move indicative of Daley's disregard for the public's right to democratically determine the future of a piece of cherished public property. In an editorial written at the time, the *Chicago Tribune* described it as an instance of "Daley's increasingly authoritarian style that brooks no disagreements, legal challenges, negotiations, compromises of any of that messy give-and-take normally associated with democratic government."[4] "The signature act of Richard Daley's 22 years in office was the midnight bulldozing of Meigs Field," wrote *Chicago Tribune* columnist Eric Zorn many years after the fact.[5] Daley surely would challenge the notion that, during the entirety of his term in office, he permitted no disagreements, legal challenges, negotiations, or compromises; nevertheless, this single example was significant enough to engender wide acceptance as representative of Daley's approach to most decisions.

The relative power of a single instance of something undesirable may reveal itself in some public policy controversies, often to the surprise of the established power structure. Stories or narratives of significant hardship, injustice, or inhumane treatment may be enough to produce consensus that policies should be changed before more analytical approaches commence to determine the extent of a problem. These narratives can be hypothetical or fictional – think of the impact of the novels *Uncle Tom's Cabin* and *The Jungle*, for example – but are more often, and unfortunately, instances of real tragedy. Instances of school shootings, deportations, human trafficking, mass transit accidents, oil spills, and so forth, may be cited with significant potency for public audiences.

Reasoning by Analogy

The final form of reasoning we will discuss is reasoning by analogy. When advocates reason by analogy, Martha Cooper writes, "the audience is asked to grasp a similarity between two apparently different phenomena in order to conclude that the characteristics common to one are also common to the other."[6] A commonly referenced analogy in the realm of public policy argumentation is the "Vietnam analogy." "Vietnam" in the Vietnam analogy has come to represent a conflict initially justified with appeals to protect a people from aggression and repression but then spirals into a protracted conflict that is unwinnable and results in needless casualties. In just about every conflict involving U.S. military intervention, those opposed to U.S. involvement have used the Vietnam analogy to argue that what occurred in the actual Vietnam conflict will occur again in the new conflict, resulting in substantial loss of life, with no end in sight, and likely a "loss" for the United States. The Vietnam analogy might emerge in the following form:

> *U.S. involvement in the Vietnam War (A) was unwise (B).*
> *U.S. involvement in Conflict X (C) is just like U.S. involvement in Vietnam (A) in all relevant respects.*
> *Therefore, U.S. involvement in Conflict X (C) would be unwise (B).*

The key to dealing with this analogical reasoning is to evaluate the comparison in the minor premise – *U.S. involvement in Conflict X (C) is just like U.S. involvement in Vietnam (A) in all relevant respects*. But, similar to the other types of reasoning considered above, we recommend first a thorough evaluation of the policy position of the advocate before contending with the analogy on which the advocate bases his or her conclusion. In the above case, the advocate is opposed to a proposal to intervene in a conflict and claims the impacts of intervention would be similar to the disastrous impacts of the Vietnam War. Whether this is a reasonable argument requires a thorough consideration of the manner in which the advocate has established a causal connection between intervention and the alleged disadvantage.

There are two types of analogies: literal and figurative.

Literal Analogies

Literal analogies compare things of the same class, such as, in the above example, two foreign policy conflicts. Literal analogies are subject to more rigorous scrutiny, and there is much guidance to the advocate seeking to establish a sound literal analogy or to invalidate a literal analogy used by others. We advise posing the following critical questions when evaluating a literal analogy:

1. Are the practices, behaviors, activities, or phenomena being compared similar enough to warrant the policy position being advocated?
2. Can the comparison be characterized as fundamentally flawed or socially offensive?

In terms of the first question, literal analogies should be practically useful, and their potential as appealing arguments should not be underestimated. They function much like examples in inductive claims, as if to argue, because it was so in that case, it will be so in this case. As such, it is practically useful to ask whether the instances are similar in all important respects and whether the comparison provides support for the goals of the advocate. The effort to invalidate an analogy, Huber and Snider write, may be aided by a consideration of the inductive and causal nature of analogies. If an analogy, for instance, cites examples that are not factual, objections pertaining to examples or inductive reasoning may be a profitable means of refuting the analogy. Huber and Snider note also that "[r]easoning by analogy is useful in supporting propositions when a policy has been tried only in a few cases – so few that induction is impossible."[7] Barbara Warnick and Edward S. Inch make a distinction between "quality" versus "quantity," concluding that a "quality comparison includes both that the comparison is of two things from the same class," and the similarities cited must be "relevant" to the claim the analogy allegedly supports.[8] In terms of quantity, they argue simply: "[t]he larger the number of relevant similarities, the more probable the conclusion."[9]

In terms of the second critical question, we observe that analogies can be rejected on two grounds: (1) they are fundamentally flawed or false, or (2) they are socially offensive. An analogy may be deemed flawed when the differences between the compared subjects outweigh the similarities. Thus, as a practical matter, you might argue that an analogy is flawed when the practices, behaviors, activities, or phenomena being compared are not similar enough to warrant the policy position being advocated. If you determine an analogy fails this test, you may adopt an abbreviated way of referring to the flawed analogy that is quite commonly used in public policy advocacy: the fallacy of the "false analogy." This is merely a label, of course, but one that has come to stand in for more elaborate lines of argument.

Analogies may also be rejected on social grounds. S. Morris Engel considers the matter of an analogy that, while it may be "sound" according to the test of logic, might be rejected because it is in bad taste. While he advises the advocate to argue, if possible, that "the fallacy lies, however, in the comparison drawn rather than in its lack of taste,"[10] both authors of this text have encountered instances when an analogy's socially inappropriate nature is the basis on which it is deemed an unworkable persuasive devise, and, as is often the case, is abandoned by its creator. In July of 1993, during the confirmation hearing for Supreme Court Justice Ruth Bader Ginsburg, Senator Orrin

Hatch (R-Utah) made an analogy between what he characterized as "judicial activism" in the opinion of the U.S. Supreme Court in *Roe v. Wade*, the 1973 case that held that a woman had a right to seek an abortion because there was a constitutional right to privacy, and an earlier (allegedly comparable) moment of judicial activism in *Dred Scott v. Sanford*, a 1857 case that held that slaves were personal property and the Fifth Amendment of the Constitution protects property owners against deprivation of their property without due process of law. Both cases, Hatch claimed, were moments when the Supreme Court created a right that did not exist in the Constitution, and thus each was a moment of "judicial activism." Hatch questioned whether Justice Ginsburg agreed. What happened next became a source of significant public and media interest, because seated alongside Hatch was a newly elected Senator from Illinois, an African American female named Carol Moseley Braun. Moseley Braun fiercely objected to the analogy on the grounds that it was offensive to her as a woman and an African American. Hatch apologized and considered an alternative means of registering the same concerns about judicial activism, even while the same analogy has been at the center of many intellectual debates over the right of judges to interpret the intent of the Constitution beyond a reading of only the words on the page.

Figurative Analogies

Figurative analogies compare things belonging to different classes, such as comparing the service you have performed on your car to regular physical exams from your physician.[11] While argumentation scholars tend to favor literal analogies when advising students to assemble the strongest appeals, figurative analogies are inevitable conventions of human communication. We advise the following critical questions be posed when contemplating figurative analogies:

1. Is the comparison offered likely to assist the advocate in his or her effort to gain the support of the audience?
2. Can the comparison be characterized as fundamentally flawed or socially offensive?

In terms of the first question, we note that figurative analogies are typically marshaled to encourage understanding of complex subjects relevant to the actual issues involved in a controversy. Warnick and Inch are very practical when discussing the potential persuasive power of figurative analogies. Of the figurative analogy, they write, "the comparison is metaphorical and illustrative rather than concrete and literal" and will "function primarily to make what is remote or poorly understood, immediate and comprehensible."[12] Thus, the primary test of a figurative analogy is one of "rhetorical effectiveness," whether the analogy causes an audience to reshape its attitudes in the direction desired by the advocate.[13]

In terms of the second critical question, we observe that figurative analogies, similar to literal analogies, can be rejected because they are fundamentally flawed, or false – when the differences between the compared subjects outweigh the similarities – or because they are socially offensive. Thus, you can determine a figurative analogy is a false analogy in the same manner in which you argue that *the practices, behaviors, activities, or phenomena being compared are not similar enough to warrant the policy position being advocated.*

It is easy to imagine socially inappropriate analogies coming in figurative forms, such as the one cited by Engel comparing the slaughter of Native Americans during the settlement of the American frontier to the adage, "you can't make an omelet without breaking a few eggs."[14]

In the next chapter, we consider the role of evidence in public policy advocacy, beginning with a theoretical discussion that focuses on how and why evidence is used in practical advocacy situations.

Exercise 5: Using Knowledge of Reasoning in a Critique of a Newspaper Opinion Piece (II)

Select a letter to the editor, column, or editorial wherein the writer is addressing a public controversy. Identify the controversy and which side of the issue the writer is on, if such can be clearly determined. Identify an instance of reasoning by deduction (categorical or disjunctive), induction, or analogy (literal or figurative). Then ask and answer the critical questions that apply to the form of reasoning.

Notes

1. Anthony Weston, *A Rulebook for Arguments* (Indianapolis: Hackett Publishing Co., 2009), 76.
2. Ibid., 76–77.
3. Robert B. Huber and Alfred C. Snider, *Influencing through Argument* (Updated Edition) (New York: International Debate Education Association, 2006), 93.
4. "A Pre-emptive Strike on Meigs," *Chicago Tribune*, April 1, 2003, accessed September 1, 2014, http://articles.chicagotribune.com/2003-04-01/news/0304010283_1_meigs-field-mayor-richard-daley-soldier-field.
5. Eric Zorn, "When the Mayor Bulldozed an Airport: Daley's Action Inspired Admiration, Outrage and Amusement," *Chicago Tribune*, April 30, 2011, accessed September 1, 2014, http://articles.chicagotribune.com/2011-04-30/news/ct-met-zorn-daley-moments-0501-201 10430_1_amusement-outrage-lakefront-airport.
6. Martha Cooper, *Analyzing Public Discourse* (Prospect Heights, IL: Waveland Press: 1989), 76.
7. Huber and Snider, 151.
8. Barbara Warnick and Edward S. Inch, *Critical Thinking and Communication: The Use of Reason in Argument*, 6th Edition (Boston: Allyn & Bacon, 2009), 116–117.
9. Ibid., 117.
10. S. Morris Engel, *With Good Reason: An Introduction to Informal Fallacies*, 2nd ed. (New York: St. Martin's Press, 1982), 129.
11. Weston, 19.
12. Warnick and Inch, 117.
13. Ibid., 117.
14. Engel, 129.

· 6 ·

THEORIES AND USES OF EVIDENCE

Takeaways

1. You have likely engaged evidence as a significant matter of concern and thus have an existing competency from which to build a sophisticated practice of evaluating evidence.
2. Unlike the subject of reasoning, the subject of evidence often arises explicitly as an issue in public advocacy. Controversies may be primarily about evidence or simply arise out of the existence of evidence.
3. Overall, the quality of evidence is more important than the credibility alone of the source or the amount of evidence marshaled. A useful general principle for considering the quality of evidence is that good evidence withstands objections.
4. Evidence marshaled by an advocate, often more so than the explicit claims made, offers you an opportunity to uncover the interests and ideologies advanced by advocates and their appeals.

Introduction

Imagine you are involved in a long-term relationship with a person who believes you may be secretly seeing another person. You will likely first ask, *"What causes them to think that?"* (or, more formally, *"What evidence points to this suspicion?"*). The accuser then tells you that *you* [1] *have been distant lately*, [2] *have been hiding your phone whenever a text message is received, and* [3] *have been defensive whenever you are asked about your whereabouts.* Moreover, you are told that [4] *a mutual friend noticed that you appear attracted to another person.* You may argue there is no evidence to support the accusation and lots of evidence to support that you have been a faithful partner. You may argue your mutual friend's suspicion is caused by his or her well-known belief that no one can be completely faithful to another person. As for being distant, protecting your phone, and being defensive, you may argue that these are highly subjective observations that, even if they were true, could point to a number of other issues that have nothing to do with whether you are being honest and faithful. The evaluation of evidence in the realm of public policy will rely on some of the same tests and objections and many more. Like the causal reasoning example from the chapter four (suggesting you and your friend go see a movie), evaluating evidence is an activity familiar to you.

In this chapter and the next, we consider evidence as a component of public policy advocacy. Similar to our discussion of reasoning, we begin by considering some theories and uses of evidence that will ground your practical engagement with evidence in the specific realm of public policy; in the chapter that follows, we introduce you to critical questions useful in considering evidence offered by authorities and in the form of statistics. First, we examine the basic components of reliable evidence that support good reasons. Second, we consider when, why, and how evidence is used in public policy advocacy. Third, we introduce you to the notion that evidence marshaled in public policy settings is intimately related to the values and ideologies of the advocate. This is a theoretical chapter intended to enhance your appreciation for the manner in which evidence operates in public policy settings, and, considering that setting generally, what you should know about evidence.

In wishing to provide you with these central lessons, we leave many standard lessons about evidence for others to provide. Other frameworks and advice are available to assist advocates in such objectives as gathering evidence and learning more about evidence from specific formats such as scholarly articles, books, newspapers, online sources, position papers, blogs, and so forth. We also do not discuss the tools and techniques used to locate such resources (the Internet, search engines, indexes, etc.), except as they relate to the changing nature of news as an authority. In the digital age, dramatic changes have occurred that have altered the way advocates locate, package, and present evidence in public policy settings. Depending on the depth of your involvement in public policy advocacy, you may wish to consider the subject of evidence beyond the guidance provided by argumentation and debate textbooks into the vast resources available within other disciplines and professional areas. The field of public administration, for example, has produced guidance on the manner in which advocates generate interest in an issue, set the agenda for policymaking bodies, determine the legislative history of an issue, and consider the appropriate format for communication (position papers, petitions and proposals, briefing memos and opinion statements, talking points, testimony within public hearings, and written public comment).[1] Most disciplines, fields, and professions have specialized standards for what is expected of practitioners attempting to justify a desired course of action. We have discussed such matters as advocacy that occurs in technical spheres, or "fields." For most advocates, experience in these fields is often required before developing a clear sense of what units of data are important when considering a particular problem within a specialized field. We suspect you have or will soon encounter a variety of such "indicators" throughout your professional lives: terms such as "shrinkage," "teacher-to-student-ratio," "consumer price index," "adherence rates," "housing starts," and so forth. Extended advocacy campaigns will expose you to the unique language, modes of reasoning, and standards of evidence preferred by advocates operating in certain technical environments.

Components of Reliable Evidence

As with evaluating reasoning, it is useful to begin with some semblance of an ideal notion of the subject of evidence. This will encourage you to consider and question assumptions you have about evidence in light of some realities of public policy advocacy settings. The result, we hope, will be a framework for considering evidence that maintains high standards for evidence use while accepting some known realities about public policy advocacy.

Ideally, evidence has a clear purpose

Generally, the purpose of evidence is to support an advocate's position. Many argumentation and debate textbooks will refer to evidence as "facts," but data comes in many forms, such as findings of studies, statistics, examples, and analogies, and not all of this information is "factual" in the purist sense of the term. In the realm of public policy, it is best to assume that no evidence is perfect, that it can always be critiqued. Whether you consider global warming or Iraq's possession of weapons of mass destruction or recurring claims about the exact state of the U.S. economy – to name a few familiar examples – public policy controversies over evidence are common even when some believe the facts are indisputable.

Evidence occupies a critical role in the performance of effective advocacy. The Toulmin model described in the prior chapter refers to evidence as "data," as noted below:[2]

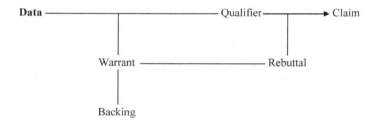

You have already learned that data are linked to a claim through reasoning, but evidence may function provocatively on its own; its purpose, therefore, will evolve as claims are made by concerned stakeholders. Data may produce immediate claims, and the infrastructure of reasoning undergirding such claims may be virtually undetectable, such as a mug shot of a neighbor charged with child sexual abuse (data) that causes a community to experience an immediate impulse to keep children far from the suspect or a video of the brutal execution of a hostage by anti-American terrorists widely viewed on the Internet (data) that causes millions to conclude military force against the captors is necessary. Therefore, it is not always clear how advocates link data to claims, but it is almost always possible to determine the data on which an advocate is basing his or her positions. Moreover, evidence often brings a controversy into existence where one may not already exist. When a study finds that African American women experience high rates of new infections of the HIV virus, for example, public health and community leaders begin a debate over the significance of such data.

Still, if you wish to improve your advocacy, you should understand the purpose of evidence deployed on either side of a policy proposition and apply a level of skepticism. Ideally, the purpose of evidence will be clear.

Ideally, evidence is of high quality

Ideally, you will look beyond the realms of personal trust and faith in the source and amount of evidence to determine the reliability of evidence. Students of public speaking often learn that information provided by speakers with high credibility – also referred to as a matter of "ethos" – is considered reliable by those who trust the source. But even a well-trusted source of evidence may have it wrong. For reasons we will explore more in this chapter, advocates may have vested interests that prevent them from adequately testing their own evidence, or cause them to set up an experiment or survey that is more likely than not to support their conclusion, or cause them to accept without proper skepticism the conclusions of others they trust – on whose research they may base their own consideration of a subject. They may also have become entrenched in a way of thinking about a subject to the point that they cannot appreciate the perspectives of others on the same matter and select only the evidence that supports goals that serve their perspective. If a source of evidence is worthy of trust – that is, worthy of your determination that their observations, conclusions, and data are credible – the evidence they offer in support of their reasons, more often than not, will prove to be reliable. As in the prior chapter, *critical questions* that are likely to be asked by the target audience can assist you in determining the quality of evidence.

Some also assume that the *more* evidence they provide, the stronger their argument becomes. It is more likely within public policy advocacy that fewer sources of support, properly selected and qualified, are sufficient (for decision makers) to establish the reasonableness of an argument. Often legislation, for example, is motivated by a single report considered highly credible or a single set of data generated by a government agency. Sometimes a preponderance of evidence is not available, and advocates must work with what they have. Consider some contemporary public policy issues where there is, arguably, little evidence. There was little evidence indicating that the U.S. invasion of Iraq would achieve its intended outcomes. The decision to invade turned on a relatively small amount of evidence, which turned out to be significantly flawed, and virtually no evidence was offered to support the advantages advocates of invasion claimed would occasion regime change. Using and critiquing evidence effectively necessitates the understanding that the strength of evidence does not rely exclusively on quantity.

Ideally, evidence withstands objections

In considering the reliability of evidence in the realm of public policy advocacy, we believe the best test for whether evidence is reliable is *whether evidence withstands objections* (recalling Martha Cooper's simple rule, "good reasons withstand objections"[3]). There is, in our view, value for you to adopt this practical guideline and to expect that others may be comfortable with much less rigorous standards – such as those that focus on the trustworthiness of the source or the amount of evidence used to support a claim. This is not to say that trustworthiness and quantity have no value in the assessment of evidence. Critical questions can focus specifically on the credibility of the source and the number of instances cited to establish a point. Your goal should be to cultivate a rigorous and practically useful approach to evaluating evidence – a comprehensive framework – for evaluating evidence that goes beyond trustworthiness of the source and quantity of evidence.

Toward that objective, it is first useful to spend some time considering when, why, and how evidence is used.

The Uses of Evidence

Today, students of argumentation and debate often consider evidence requirements in relation to the stock issues or the burdens of advocates contending with controversies. We discussed stock issues in chapter three; in this chapter, we consider the manner in which evidence functions to support an advocate's *establishment of* – in the case of the affirmative – or *challenge of* – in the case of the negative – *the problem, the cause, the solution, and the advantages*. Robert Newman and Dale Newman, in their seminal text, *Evidence*, described three primary ways evidence is used in the practice of policy advocacy in terms that help illustrate why evidence is critical to these objectives: to support approving or disapproving assessments of the status quo, to support policy goals, and to support predictions. Consistent with the structure of stock issues, Newman and Newman note that approving or disapproving assessments of the status quo will often occur first, and so we shall consider first the use of evidence to support descriptions of what we refer to as an insufficient or sufficient status quo.[4]

Evidence to Support Descriptions of an Insufficient or Sufficient Status Quo

Evidence used to describe and assess the status quo pertains to the stock issues of both problem and cause. Affirmative advocates maintain that a significant problem, worth correcting, is caused by something in the status quo; negative advocates claim that the status quo is not causing a problem or that the problem is not significant enough to warrant a change (or risk disadvantages that will occur as a consequence of the solution being advocated). Newman and Newman refer to such descriptions of the status quo as "positional statements," which they note, more simply, is the answer to the question, *Where are we now?*[5] We recommend describing the status quo as either "sufficient" or "insufficient." In chapter three, we discussed the problem and the cause as essential stock issues, a cause-and-effect relationship that must be addressed by the advocate of a policy proposal, and we outlined four types of barriers that prevent the present system from correcting itself (structural inherency, attitudinal inherency, philosophical inherency and existential inherency). When affirmative advocates use evidence to establish *where we are*, they describe a system that requires adjustment in order to prevent a continuation of some undesirable effect (an insufficient status quo), often injustice, unfairness, preventable suffering, and so forth. That is, *if you are seeking a change in the present system*, you will use evidence to establish that a problem exists in the status quo. In response, negative advocates may also use evidence to describe a status quo that either produces no harms or produces the fewest amount of harms possible given the challenges of dealing with a respective problem in the status quo (a sufficient status quo). That is, *if you are seeking to maintain the status quo*, you will use evidence to challenge the existence of an alleged problem within the status quo or that such a problem is significant.

In late 2013, at the center of debate over whether the United States should intervene in the civil war in Syria, advocates on both sides debated the reliability of evidence concerning the status quo. Were chemical weapons used to kill civilians? How many civilians died? Was the Syrian government led by Bashar al-Assad responsible? The Obama administration's answers to these questions described an insufficient status quo: a system that permitted the use of chemical weapons by governments against their own people and a system that may lack the resolve to address such atrocities. Those opposed to a U.S. strike against the Syrian regime offered different answers to these questions, such as the claim by Russia's President Vladimir Putin, that evidence pointed to the possibility that the Syrian opposition forces fired chemical weapons on innocent civilians in order to encourage U.S. involvement against the Syrian regime. Some opposed to a U.S. strike also agreed with part of the Obama administration's description of the status quo. Economist and political commentator Robert Reich, following President Barack Obama's September 5, 2013, speech regarding the alleged use of chemical weapons by Syria, wrote an intentionally abbreviated assessment of the Syrian conflict, offering an example of an advocate describing the status quo:

> Cliff notes on a potentially disastrous decision. (1) Were Syrian civilians killed by chemical weapons? Yes. (2) How many? Estimates vary. (3) Was Assad responsible? Probably but not definitely.[6]

For Reich, the status quo also involved another viable option short of a U.S. military strike: economic sanctions and a freeze on Syrian assets.

Evidence to Describe or Outline the Solution

If the stock issues of problem and cause answer the question, "*Where are we now?*", the *solution* is the answer to the question, "*What do we want to accomplish?*" Affirmative advocates use evidence to describe or outline the specifics of a solution or policy. Negative advocates use evidence to argue that a proposed solution will fail to reduce or eliminate the problem described by affirmative advocates or support their claim that a proposed solution will cause disadvantages uniquely caused by the proposed policy change. In either case, evidence will generally be used to describe *what policy is being pursued*, or what Newman and Newman term the "policy goal." To this end, according to Newman and Newman, evidence will be used to establish (1) the facts supporting the goal, (2) whether the goal can be sought consistently, and (3) what costs are associated with achieving the goal.[7]

In referring to "facts supporting the goal," Newman and Newman discuss a wide variety of facts that might be offered to establish that a goal is *grounded* in something.[8] Grounds are commonly defined as "factors forming a basis for action or the justification for a belief;" thus, to "be grounded in" something means to give something abstract a firm theoretical or practical basis.[9] If the goal is to meet the obligations of the United States to stand up to dictators who use weapons of mass destruction against innocent civilians, some facts must be cited to establish that such obligations exist, that the targeted regime is a dictatorship, that the regime is indeed responsible for an alleged act of aggression, and/or that international laws have been violated. For this pur-pose, an obligation to intervene would be grounded in treaties or internation-al law, a United Nations resolution, and so forth, in which case the relevant clauses of such documents would be the evidence. Reports of neutral agencies based on eyewitness accounts and surveillance or highly credible documenta-tion of war crimes would likely also be required.

Whether a goal can be pursued consistently is a matter of asking whether a justification for a goal is consistent with prior motivations of advocates and the outcomes they predicted in similar cases and whether the same goals have been, and can be, applied in similar situations. Consistency is an im-portant value within democratic decision-making societies; in tyrannies or dictatorships, which provide little to no role for public input and approval of decisions, whether a policy goal can be pursued consistently is less import-ant. Consider the question of consistency raised as a prominent criticism in late August 2013, when U.S. President Barack Obama called on Congress to authorize a strike against government facilities in Syria. Obama's justification, that the use of chemical weapons constituted the crossing of a "red line" that could not be ignored by the international community, was questioned, partic-ularly by Iranians, who recalled Saddam Hussein's use of mustard gas in Hal-abja in 1988, wherein more than 3,000 Kurds died. The United States, then an ally of Iraq and enemy of Iran, took no action in response to that chemical weapons attack. More troubling, the United States, argue many, ignored the repeated use of chemical weapons by Iraq in the Iran-Iraq War in the 1980s. In early September 2013, former Iranian official Seyed Hossein Mousavi-an, a research scholar at the Princeton University Woodrow Wilson School, explained how the Iranian people might react to U.S. military action in Syria:

> They cannot imagine the issue is chemical weapons, because Saddam Hussein used chemical weapons with the support of the U.S. against Iran in the war. [In] 1982–1988, 100,000 Iranians, they were killed, or injured by chemical weapons where and when materials and technology was provided by the U.S. For Iranians, they cannot imagine, really, the issue is chemical weapons. The U.S. has used nuclear weapons. The U.S. has supported Saddam for the use of chemical weapons. Now they say 1,400 people, they have been killed through the use of chemical weapons in Syria, it's really disaster. But more disaster was the time 100,000 Iranians, they were killed during the war and the U.S. supported Saddam.[10]

For Mousavian, these facts of history meant that Obama's policy goal could not be sought consistently, and they suggested there must be some other main policy objective driving intervention in the Syrian affair, such as re-gime change in Syria. Consistency is a frequent standard evoked by political leaders, typically taking the form of affirmative advocates claiming their solution is consistent with prior approaches taken in similar situations and negative advocates claiming a proposed policy is inconsistent with prior actions.

"Costs" concern undesirable consequences of a policy, which may include actual monetary costs of the plan and/or what are commonly referred to as "disadvantages." As we note in our discussion of the fifth critical question associated with causal reasoning (*Will the proposed solution cause additional problems or disadvantages not already occurring in the status quo?*), disadvantages are typically advanced by negative advocates. Staying within the same public policy issue, the question of whether the United States should strike Syrian government targets prompted economist and political commentator Robert Reich to outline, in a Facebook post, several disadvantages of using military force (number 7, letters a through g below):

> Cliff notes on a potentially disastrous decision. (1) Were Syrian civilians killed by chemical weapons? Yes. (2) How many? Estimates vary. (3) Was Assad responsible? Probably but not definitely. (4) Should the world respond? Yes. (5) What's the best response? Economic sanctions and a freeze on Syrian assets. (6) What are the advantages of bombing Syria with missiles? (a) Highly visible response, (b) no American troops on the ground. *(7)What are the disadvantages?* (a) Syrian civilians will inevitably be killed, (b) it will fuel more anti-American, anti-Western sentiment, thereby increasing the ranks of terrorists in Syria and elsewhere in the Middle East, (c) our involvement will escalate if Assad or others use additional chemical weapons or engage in retribution against the us or Israel, (d) we have no exit strategy, (e) most of our allies aren't with us, and we can't be the world's policeman everywhere, (f) it will distract us from critical problems at home, (g) the Syrian rebels are not our friends. (8) So why is Obama pursuing this so vigorously? (Your theory?). [emphasis added][11]

Claims that costs or disadvantages will accompany a public policy proposal are occasions for offering and engaging evidence. Just as affirmative advocates must establish that the goal is grounded in evidence and can be pursued consistently, presumably they also must evaluate the costs of such policy. However, in public policy advocacy, rarely would a proponent of a policy bring costs up for con-sideration; instead, it is typically the prerogative of the target audience and opposition to raise the costs of a policy goal, as the above example illustrates. Similar to the prior example, Reich does not believe the advantages outweigh the disadvantages, prompting him to suggest some other motivation must be driving the Obama administration. But, costs are not always unintended or undesirable to advocates of a policy goal. Often advocates know they are advancing one interest over another, have weighed the relative benefits against the costs, and are willing to address the costs as part of their advocacy in favor of a policy.

Evidence to Support Predictions

In the prior chapters, we noted that public policy advocacy is, fundamentally, an enterprise of prediction, and we focused on the critical questions target audiences and advocates ask when predictions are made. Newman and Newman devote an entire chapter of their text to "Supporting Predictions" and isolating forms of policy prediction commonly supported with evidence. Predictions in public policy advocacy typically come in the form of advantages (the fourth stock issue). "To give a good reason for adopting a certain policy," write Newman and Newman, "involves providing evidence that the policy will have desirable consequences, that it will gain more than it costs."[12] However, negative advocates will also provide evidence to support predictions, either to prove that a proposed solution will fail to realize its claimed advantages or will lead to undesirable consequences or disadvantages.

The Role of Ideology in the Evaluation of Evidence

Beyond developing an appreciation for the function of evidence in relation to the stock issues of policy advocacy, we advise advocates to pay close attention to the manner in which an advocate's use of evidence may reveal his or her values or what also might be called his or her ideology. In his early work and beyond, Robert Newman devoted his scholarly career to the consideration of what he and *Evidence* co-author Dale Newman refer to as "bias."[13] Bias, the writers claim, function as "a set of lenses which focuses the attention of an observer so that he [or she] perceives certain phenomena and disregards others, thus distorting reality."[14] They draw a distinction between "perceptual distortions" – strong biases that render the generator, user, or consumer of evidence either incapable of perceiving something that is plainly evident or perceiving something that is not supported by the evidence[15] – and "willful distortions" – bias that is so strong that the generator or user of evidence aims to intentionally mislead or lie.[16]

In a later analysis of foreign policy decision making, Newman argues that, "[w]hat primarily distinguishes policy argument is the necessary factoring into all policy arguments of human goals and values."[17] Something of a model begins to take shape in Newman's work, as he directs us to consider both a "value premise" and corresponding prediction advanced by an advocate as a means of unmasking the ideological interests of an advocate. He cites arguments made by those opposed to an air strike against Soviet missile installations in Cuba when the issue was discussed among President John F. Kennedy and his advisors on October 17, 1962:

> Value premise: The United States should uphold its traditions.
> Prediction: A surprise air strike would be, and would be perceived to be, in conflict with those traditions.[18]

The practical lesson for public policy advocates is to decipher the value premise and prediction in order to identify the underlying ideological position held by an advocate and to appreciate the effect this ideological position has on the quality of evidence selected (or developed) to support an advocate's policy goals.

The values and ideologies driving claims and evidence selection can be tricky to analyze, because, like so many dimensions of public policy advocacy, the key value behind a claim is often difficult to detect and may be intentionally concealed. If, for example, you are advocating that your employer provide staff in same-sex domestic partnerships the same benefits provided to married opposite-sex couples (what we will call "equitable coverage"), responses may involve a variety of evidence that offers no clear indication of a value- or morals-based objection, such as an illustration that proves the employer's policy is consistent with policies of similar employers. The process of determining what you might argue depends significantly on your assessment of the opponent's values. Taken on face value, the opponent appears to value consistency, and this may indeed be true, but other values influencing his or her argument may become clear during further discussion. Eventually, you may encounter evidence added to the debate that is clearly produced by a conservative political organization that promotes marriage between one man and one woman as the most effective and safe family structure. From this evidence, you may discern that the opposition values traditional family structure and/or harbors personal anxieties about same-sex relationships and the social consequences they foresee from granting equitable coverage. The resulting value premise and prediction would be something like the following:

Value premise: The most effective and safe family structure involves a marriage between one man and one woman, and employers should not encourage same-sex relationships.
Prediction: Providing equitable coverage will encourage same-sex relationships and attract homosexuals and their radical politics.

In this case, your focus would have to shift to exposing the bias of the source and noting the nature in which the materials exaggerate the impacts of equitable coverage on the social environment of a workplace.

In addition to the type or sources of evidence advocates select to support their claims, values and ideologies are often revealed through terms advocates use (rhetorical scholar Michael Calvin McGee refers to such terms as "ideographs"[19]) or their affiliations, such as organizations for which advocates work or to which they belong, or scholars with whom advocates have worked. Assessing an advocate's goals, values, and predictions, therefore, is a wise endeavor to the extent you are capable of learning or deducing such factors.

In the next chapter, we review critical questions you can use to evaluate evidence offered by authorities and when offered in the specific form of statistics.

Exercise 6: Do the Facts Support the Goal?

Identify a contemporary example in which evidence is expected to support an overarching policy goal. Identify the predictions cited as justifications for the policy proposal and describe how evidence is used to support those predictions. Identify what alternative routes of addressing the problem exist (either your own ideas or ideas being discussed within the controversy). What evidence is available that suggests such an alternative means of addressing the problem would succeed? Is there evidence to suggest that such an alternative may fail to address the problem?

Notes

1. See Catherine F. Smith, *Writing Public Policy: A Practical Guide to Communicating in the Policy Making Process* (Oxford: Oxford University Press, 2010); see also Karen Bogenschneider and Thomas J. Corbett, *Evidence-Based Policymaking: Insights from Policy-Minded Researchers and Research-Minded Policymakers* (New York: Routledge, 2010).
2. Stephen Toulmin, *The Uses of Argument*, rev. ed. (Cambridge: Cambridge University Press, 2003).
3. Martha Cooper, *Analyzing Public Discourse* (Prospect Heights, IL: Waveland Press, 1989), 117.
4. Robert P. Newman and Dale R. Newman, *Evidence* (Boston: Houghton Mifflin Company, 1969), 16.
5. Ibid., 16.
6. Robert Reich's Facebook page, accessed September 5, 2013, https://www.facebook.com/RBReich/posts/660416167304316.
7. Ibid., 6.
8. Ibid., 6.
9. Elizabeth J. Jewell and Frank Abate, Eds., *The New Oxford American Dictionary* (Oxford: Oxford University Press, 2001), 750–751.
10. Marco Werman, *How Iran Might Respond to a Military Strike on Syria*, September 3, 2013. PRI Audio, 4:50. Accessed September 1, 2014, http://www.theworld.org/2013/09/iran-response-syria-strike/.
11. Robert Reich's Facebook page, accessed September 5, 2013, https://www.facebook.com/RBReich/posts/660416167304316.
12. Newman and Newman, 33.
13. Robert Newman's focus on ideology and evidence began with his 1961 extended study of whether the United States should recognize communist China (Robert P. Newman, *Recognition of Communist China: A Concise, Complete, and Readable Summing-Up of the Major Issues* (New York: Macmillan, 1961). Following the subsequent *Evidence* with Dale Newman, Robert devoted his entire career to, in the words of David Deifell, "acclaiming the available evidence that should have held sway and decrying the ideologies that compelled people to ignore it" (Robert P. Newman and David Deifell, *Invincible Ignorance in American Foreign Policy* (New York: Peter Lang, 2013), 166).
14. Newman and Newman, 58.
15. Ibid., 58.
16. Ibid., 66.
17. Robert R. Newman, "Foreign Policy: Decision and Argument," *Advances in Argumentation Theory and Research*, J. Robert Cox and Charles Arthur Willard, Eds. (Carbondale: Southern Illinois University Press, 1982), 320.
18. Ibid., 328.
19. Michael Calvin McGee, "The 'Ideograph': A Link between Rhetoric and Ideology," *Quarterly Journal of Speech*, 66 (1980), 1–16.

· 7 ·

EVALUATING EVIDENCE

Takeaways

1. A relatively short list of critical questions can be marshaled to consider evidence, and posing these questions will address the most common general categories under which a variety of evidence is considered in the practice of public policy advocacy – authorities and statistics.
2. The Internet has had a significant impact on the manner in which evidence is evaluated. This impact is more a matter to be appreciated at particular engagement points with evidence than something that can be understood fully.
3. Beyond the general applicability of the critical questions, several source-specific considerations are useful in evaluating evidence derived from the news media and scholarship.

Introduction

In this chapter, we provide a framework for evaluating evidence, focusing on evidence offered by authorities and within the specific form of statistics. Determining whether evidence is more or less reliable begins with considering *who the source is* and *what is being offered*. We refer to the *who* as "authorities." In terms of *what*, we have in mind a wide variety of labels used to describe the types or forms of evidence under consideration (testimony, statistics, examples, scholarship, documents, news, secondary sources, etc.). As a practical matter, your vantage point is also important. Are you evaluating *your own use of evidence* or *another's use of evidence*? Consider the following hypothetical example: At a city planning commission meeting, imagine you belong to a local not-for-profit organization that wishes to erect a large sign with a digital screen that displays video outside of your headquarters. A resident opposed to the sign testifies to the commission that a driver recently involved in an accident in a nearby town claimed that he was distracted by a large video sign. What would be your response? After reading this chapter, you might claim that neither the driver nor the resident possess the expertise to determine whether a large video sign caused the driver's accident. Moreover, you might also point out that the resident did not hear the complaint of the driver firsthand (that it is "secondhand" information). Or, you might offer a study performed by a sign manufacturers' association indicating that no findings support that traffic accidents can be linked to digital signs. The resident might then counter that you are not citing a study but a newspaper article that discusses the position of the manufacturers' association, generally, and not specific to your city ("The source," argues the resident, "is a secondary source"). The resident might also argue that the manufacturers' association has a substantial material bias in the conclusion. Concluding that digital screens are safe may serve to substantially benefit manufacturers of digital signs. The resident might go further to argue, as you did, that the authors of the report cited in the newspaper article did not perform a study or that their study was structured in such a way that was unscientific and unrepresentative. Weaved into this dispute are a wide range of claims made about evidence, each dependent to a large extent on the vantage point of the advocate. Consideration of who offers evidence, what specifically they offer, and from which vantage point you are considering the evidence focuses attention, ideally, in a productive manner.

    In this chapter, we provide a relatively short list of critical questions you can use to consider evidence, to address the most common general categories under which a variety of evidence is considered in the practice of public policy advocacy – authorities and statistics. Our intention is to spark your thinking about these issues, not to offer a complete framework for evaluating all information. In discussing evidence from authorities, we also provide source-specific consideration for the evaluation of news media and scholarship.

Authorities

Authorities are *who* said or wrote what is being used to support a claim. Using the term "authorities," we refer to how they, as sources of evidence, function in society. To determine what type of authority is offering information and to begin to evaluate the information as evidence, we recommend the following initial general question:

> To what particular profession or community does the authority belong that causes the authority to offer information?

The phrase "causes the authority to offer information" is packed with meaning. The idea of an authority having cause to offer information should trigger a critical posture whereby you are considering a variety of factors that led to the generation of knowledge and willingness/desire to share it. You are, in effect, asking whether the authority is offering information about which it can claim to possess some level of expertise, deeper understanding, or experience upon which to base its conclusions. Through this initial question, your close evaluation of evidence provided by authorities begins.

Evaluating Evidence from Authorities

Similar to the analysis of reasoning, we recommend that you pose *critical questions* when considering evidence. Systems for evaluating evidence are processes that determine whether a source and the content of a source's conclusions are *reliable*. We recommend some relatively basic critical questions that can permit you to exercise more control over the manner in which evidence is used in public policy advocacy – whether this concerns your own evidence or the evidence used by others.

Those evaluating the reliability of authorities should ask (and, in the case of the public audience, will likely ask) the following five critical questions:

1. Is the authority known?
2. Does the information offered by the authority support the claim?
3. Is the authority capable of observing the phenomenon the authority claims to understand?
4. Is the information offered by the authority likely to be affected by bias?
5. Is the information offered by the authority accurate?

The first critical question concerns the clear identification of the authority. For an authority to be influential on the audience's thinking, it must be clearly identified. "Scientists say …" or even the more commonly used "They say…" are *always* insufficient references. In everyday communication, it may be appropriate to indicate that you heard a report on NBC News, but in public policy advocacy, additional details of the report would be expected so that an authority is identified and can be evaluated for its capacity to observe the phenomenon about which it is reporting, possible bias, and accuracy.

The second critical question is one of the most basic in the practice of argumentation and debate: whether the information provided by the authority supports the claim it is intended to support. An authority must also be used appropriately to support a claim being made by an advocate. While this is a very basic question, the answer provided to it is not. It is not enough to simply say that the information does or does not support the claim. If you are challenging the authority on this level, you must indicate how the claim and the information offered by the authority differ. Typically, this is done in tandem with the third critical question, because you must focus on what is being observed by the authority and note that it is not the same as, or differs in significant ways from, the subject matter of the claim. You may also need to focus on the terms used by the advocate versus those used by the authority. Whereas the advocate's claim is "Russia will initiate a nuclear attack," for example, you would surely be correct to protest if the authority offers only that "Russia, a nuclear power, has reacted with hostility when states along its border are on the brink of revolution." If you are selecting an authority to support your claim, our recommendation is to let the authority's particular claims and language guide your writing of the claims you are constructing.

The third critical question concerns whether the authority is capable of observing the phenomenon the authority claims to understand. This is a question of *capacity*, or more-precisely labeled by Newman and Newman as "perceptual capacity."[1] Capacity is most often a matter of training in procedures that produce bias-free or objective conclusions. A molecular biologist is trained to observe phenomena others cannot observe. While noting that all areas of expertise are unique, Newman and Newman generally conclude that experts:

(1) should have training and expertise in the area under study,
(2) know relevant languages and technical jargon, and
(3) have a genuine intellectual curiosity about what they are observing.[2]

Capacity is relatively easy to determine within areas of expertise that are associated with collegiate disciplines and professional fields. It is more challenging to determine capacity in areas of "expertise" that are less recognized or unregulated. One can become certified in a variety of fields by purchasing accreditation through professional associations and/or after relatively short online tutorials and exams. Authorities may also derive their capacity through many years of work within occupations or organizations for which no credentialing process occurs.

The fourth critical question concerns bias. The question of bias or subjectivity is captured in a concept explored by Newman and Newman, labeled "perceptual distortion," which they define as "a bias, belief system, or perspective" that acts as "a set of lenses which focuses the attention of an observer" so that he or she "perceives certain phenomena and disregards others, thus distorting reality."[3] Identifying bias begins by classifying a bias as either caused by ideology, national interest, self-interest, unconscious partisanship, or power, according to Newman and Newman. Robert James Branham simplifies these categories further, explaining that there are three basic sources of biases:

(a) having a *material stake* in the outcome of a dispute.
(b) having an *ego investment* in the matter.
(c) having an *ideological stake* or perspective sufficient to distort one's judgment or expression.[4]

Perceptual distortions that might be caused by economic or material interests may not always be visible. *Who is being paid to write what by whom?* is a useful question to determine whether an authority has an economic interest sufficient enough to render his or her perception unreliable. Bias of a material nature would include employment and career considerations as well – *How might an authority's conclusions be affected by how it – in the case of an organization – derives revenue, or he or she – in the case of a person – derives income?*

Somewhat related to such economic concerns, Newman and Newman argue that scholars and others who originate ideas and steward theories through the development and publication process can be affected by "a parental affection" for their work.[5] Branham refers to this form of bias as an "ego investment," a desire to receive credit or praise for an achievement.[6] Advocates evaluating evidence affected by this form of bias tend to exaggerate moments when their conclusions are confirmed and minimize or ignore moments when their conclusions are proven to be unreliable.[7]

In the prior chapter, we discussed the role of ideology in public policy advocacy. Within the critical question framework we recommend in this chapter, ideology figures as a matter of bias. Newman and Newman cite ideology as the most potent factor that distorts perceptions.[8] Contemporary examples of the types of identifications that signal bias might include "Tea Partiers," "neoconservatives," "Jihadists," "advocates of gun control," "creationists," and so forth. In the case of all forms of bias, it is important to remember that an authority's mere association to persons or institutions does not constitute a bias sufficient to distort a judgment or perspective. You may find it useful to further determine whether a recognizable or suspected bias is (1) relevant to the subject matter under consideration by the authority (the subject about which the authority is addressing) and (2) evident in the specific material (the specific information offered by the authority).

A final matter related to bias considers the advantages of bias, in this case reluctant observations. Newman and Newman introduce a basic evidence standard, or indicator of credibility, that holds that "[t]he greater the damage of his [or her] own testimony to a witness, the more credible it is."[9] On a practical level, the discovery of a reluctant authority can provide an advocate a significant advantage over his or her opponent. Typically, that the authority is reluctant is a matter of conjecture on the part of the advocate using the authority to support a claim. The advocate might say, "Even George W. Bush, not exactly a 'dove' when it comes to the use of the U.S. military, is opposed to intervention in the Syrian civil war." Rarely do authorities admit that their latest conclusions on a matter about which they have previously spoken or written represents a reversal in their thinking. Where such shifts in thinking or findings do occur, however, they can offer significant support for courses of action that are highly controversial. For example, during 2012 and 2013, several conservative Republican political figures announced publically that they could no longer support the denial of marriage equality to same-sex couples. As converts, their positions on such issues as same-sex adoption and the fundamental right of all Americans to marry the one they love surfaced as support for the marriage equality platform and legal argument.

The fifth critical question concerns the accuracy of the information provided. First, authorities may "get it wrong" because of limited perceptual capacity, but this is not the same as *intentionally* misleading or offering information which they know to be untrue. There are times when authorities can be said to deliberately report something they know to be untrue. Newman and Newman refer to this as "willful distortion."[10] In simple terms, willful distortion is a lie, and the assumption behind the use of this label is always that the authority is aware if the lie. Willful distortions are most often motivated by the same biases discussed above, and they are more common, according to Newman and Newman, when tensions are high and are likely to be repeated by the same authority over time. Regardless of the reason behind or frequency of willful distortions, for the student of evidence, willful distortions are no different than false information generated due to a perceptual distortion: both must be rejected as unreliable. The fifth critical question might also identify a "nonauthentic" or "fraudulent" document.[11] An inauthentic document is essentially one that does not really come from the source alleged. Thus, a fabricated or plagiarized document is considered inauthentic.

Source-Specific Considerations

Authorities belonging to particular professions or sectors of society are more or less prone to certain flaws concerning evidence use. In their 1969 text, Newman and Newman provide a comprehensive review of the government, the press, pressure groups, and professional scholars, arguing that the conclusions of these sources require particular skepticism and deserve more or less respect according to several source-specific standards.[12] Of these four, we wish to offer some updated guidance concerning the news media and scholarship.

News Media

Much has been written about the news media and the reliability of information offered by news sources. Internet sources of news have increasingly replaced printed news outlets and altered the character of broadcast news significantly. The consolidation of American news corporations into large publically traded corporations seeking to reduce costs (and maximize profits) has had a direct impact on the amount of time reporters can spend within the proximity of the activity about which they are expected to report. Alex S. Jones documents the precipitous decline of news that has as its purpose to hold those with power accountable.[13] What this means for those evaluating the use of evidence (their own or others' evidence) is an open question for scholars, students, and practitioners of public policy advocacy.

For the most part, the critical questions will provide you with profitable tools for evaluating the reliability of news. The question of bias is perhaps the most important critical test you should apply to news media, whether it is traditional print news, television news, or news found online. Asking whether the information you acquire is even intended to be news may serve as a starting point in assessing perceptual distortion. A search for the latest news on the "causes of obesity" will instantly offer links to a myriad of websites owned and operated by manufacturers of weight loss products and or providers of weight loss services. The factual information about nutrition and weight loss provided in such formats may appear perfectly reasonable, be consistent with general consensus, and be backed by the testimony of authorities with impressive credentials. Posing the critical questions to challenge evidence from authorities, however, should cause serious concerns about the reliability of such information, depending on the claims you are considering.

While the news media continues to generate a significant amount of information, when seeking evidence to support your claims, you must carefully assess the quality of that information. That task is challenging in several respects. First, as noted by Jones, many who have always gone online for information have not developed the "news habit."[14] Young Americans do not generally engage in a routine effort to acquire the news.[15] If you are one who rarely consults news in any form, you will find the evaluation of evidence used in news, or news used as evidence, regardless of the means used to find it, to be particularly challenging. You may be particularly attracted to blog or Facebook posts that provide information on topics that concern you personally, but you may not regularly consult a news service to learn what is occurring in terms of domestic and foreign affairs (subjects of public policy). For example, imagine you are personally concerned about the progress of immigration reform, and you read a post written by a pro-reform advocate you are following on Facebook who alleges that rules the Obama administration put in place to prevent deportation of individuals brought to the United States illegally by their parents are in jeopardy because of Congressional action. You may view this information as reliable, even if you have little to no idea what Congressional action has occurred or know little about the advocate making the claim. After some inquiry, you may find that such concern was prompted by a single representative or senator introducing an amendment that has no chance of passing – a common occurrence in the legislative branches of the United States.

Second, it is not always clear who the authority is. In evaluating news, you must first determine *who is the "authority" to which you will apply the critical questions?* Is it the author of the information you are evaluating? Or, is it an authority referred to in the article or posting? Once you have determined who the authority is, the standard questions would apply. Most likely news sources will not answer those questions for you; you will need to consider the news content carefully.

Third, it is often difficult to distinguish between authentic news and information produced for other reasons. Today, in the era of inexpensive means of video production and ample opportunities to post information online, it is easier for institutions, individuals, and organizations to release information as fully packaged stories that are reposted and linked in accordance with social affiliations and political perspectives. We have personally encountered family members and friends who were excited to share with us provocative conspiracy theories offered in attractive documentary formats online. Whether such material relied on authentic material or could itself be considered authentic material is a highly relevant question for the student of evidence.

Finally, the common notion that primary sources are more credible than secondary sources is complicated when applied to online news. The value of a primary source lies in your ability to evaluate it more closely than you can a secondary source. Yet, so much of online news aggregates and consolidates the experience, observations, and opinions of those who have generally come to be viewed as primary sources. It is reasonable to favor news reports that rely on primary sources; however, according primary sources more respect may cause you to apply insufficient scrutiny to the plentiful primary sources available online, because almost anyone can function like a journalist online (what is sometimes referred to as "citizen journalism"[16]). You will need to be especially cautious when selecting information offered by ordinary people claiming to know something that others may wish to know.

Scholarship

By most standards, scholars are considered the most reliable sources of evidence. Scholars are expected to follow "scholarly methods" to validate their claims within their particular fields of expertise. Historians are expected to use the "historical method" and scientists the "scientific method," for example.

Such methods are conventional practices for accruing knowledge within a discipline and permitting verification (so that other scholars can confirm the findings if they follow the same method). Due to their training and commitment to these methods, the conclusions of scholars are viewed to be superior to those of non-scholars.[17]

The nature of shared scholarly research is relevant to the prestige of scholars. Scholars formally share the findings of their research through specialized journals (referred to as "scholarly journals") affiliated with their disciplines or in the form of book-length work published by academic or university presses. In either case, the work is typically "peer reviewed" or "refereed" by an editor and several reviewers who, in order to avoid bias, do not know who the author is. Acceptance of the final product is contingent on the approval of these "blind" reviews, which often comes only after substantial revisions have occurred so that the final product conforms to the highest standards of excellence in the discipline in which the scholar belongs. These steps are not always followed in each instance a scholar writes something and shares it with others. Scholars, like anyone, can post an opinion in a journalistic format or online. Increasingly, scholars have developed blogs to post their views and cultivate professional associations with other scholars. These interactive formats often seed a scholar's formal research agenda, but such writings are not subject to the same peer review that precedes the formal publishing of scholarship intended for an academic audience.

While scholarship can be highly reliable as evidence, it presents you with several unique challenges. First, you may find scholarship difficult to comprehend and require a general introduction to research processes before properly discerning what portions of a scholarly work should be cited as evidence to support a claim. Most scholarship commences with either a research question or hypothesis. Some form of review of what others have written on the subject may appear before or after the research question or hypothesis, which may be brief but linked to citations in the form of footnotes or endnotes, with which the scholar may agree or disagree. A "methodology" for answering the research question or testing the hypothesis is almost always explained, in some instances in very formal, complex sections of a work of scholarship. The "meat" of scholarship for you is typically the "findings," which are offered in some form of a "discussion." Some scholars end their writing with "implications," concluding remarks about what the findings may suggest about related matters and the direction in which the research might be expanded. The "findings" or "discussion" is where you will find the most useful material to cite as evidence, whereas the other material is written principally to explain the technical steps the scholar took to perform the research. Within the specialized field of scholarship, disagreements may arise also over the methodology employed, which, some might argue, was flawed and therefore produced a flawed conclusion.

Second, it is difficult to disqualify scholarship. Typically, scholarship is discounted with alternative conclusions offered by other scholars with expertise in the same areas. Scholarship often exists for this very reason, as generations of scholars rethink prior conclusions and exploit the potential of new technologies to generate new knowledge. In most advocacy situations in which scholarship is used as evidence by your opponent, you will find yourself offering alternative scholarship and leaving the audience to sort out the relative value of either side's evidence. It is far more challenging for non-scholars to effectively discredit scholarship. One of the most effective routes for non-scholars to address the complex conclusions of scholars is to illuminate ideological biases of scholars. Otherwise, non-scholars must assume the burdens associated with the methodologies used to produce the scholarship. Discrediting a conclusion by a historian, for example, might require bringing to the surface archival documents the historian ignored in assembling his or her conclusions, which would require extensive research.

Third, you often must distinguish between scholarship and opinion that is buoyed by the strength of a scholar's authority and reputation. The question you should ask is not whether the source is a scholar, per se, but *whether the evidence is, indeed, scholarship produced through a scholarly method and peer review* or whether it is more appropriately considered journalism, blogging, or simply an individual's perspective. For example, the opinion of Robert Reich on the prospect of a U.S. military strike on government facilities in Syria is not scholarship, even though Reich would be considered by most to be a scholar. Reich is a lawyer by trade who became a government official during the administration of Jimmy Carter, then a professor at the John F. Kennedy School of Government at Harvard University, and then the Secretary of Labor under Bill Clinton. Today, as a professor of public policy at the University of California, Berkeley, Reich's areas of expertise can be found listed on his faculty webpage, but among the listed areas you will *not* find American foreign policy, international relations, American national security, or the politics of the Middle East. Thus, as wise as a reader may believe Reich is, as much as he or she may respect him for his books and recognition as a professor, and as much as he or she may agree with his conclusions on any subject, Reich's perspective on the Syrian conflict is not scholarship. Asking whether a scholar's work is scholarship is tantamount to registering objections concerning whether the authority possesses the perceptual capacity to accurately observe a phenomenon under consideration.

Finally, it is challenging to present scholarship to decision makers. Scholarship is written for other scholars, rarely for policymakers. Karen Bogenschneider and Thomas J. Corbett, in their book-length consideration of the subject of evidence-based policymaking, note that policymakers almost always prefer presentations that provide an opportunity to discuss research rather than written material,[18] suggesting that it is better to have a scholar present his or her own findings or translate the finding of another scholar than to provide written materials and expect a decision maker to review them. If that is not possible, research presented to policymakers must pass what they refer to as an "accessibility test," which amounts to brief summaries, understandably written.[19]

Statistics

Statistics are almost immediately respected in public policy advocacy. In our experience as teachers of argument, debate coaches, and practitioners of public policy advocacy, if statistics appear related to the subject being discussed, they are afforded a level of respect above whatever else may be offered. The most important point to make about statistics is that such numbers, as a type of evidence, should be subject to the same level of skepticism as evidence offered by authorities.

You do not need to be an expert in mathematics to use or effectively evaluate statistics. You merely need to be observant. Quantitative literacy should be the goal of any person with a serious interest in public policy, but it is an evolving skill that comes with study and experience with data in the workplace and public service. In considering statistical data, Newman and Newman advise the asking of three critical questions:

(1) Who wants to prove what?
(2) What do the figures really represent?
(3) What conclusions do the figures support?[20]

The first question overlaps with our discussion of evidence offered by authorities, and we have explored extensively the critical questions you should pose in that regard.

The second question – *What do the figures really represent?* – is less a question of who the source is and more a matter of understanding how the statistical data are produced. Statistics may be simple numbers, percentages, averages, high scores, low scores, and so forth, or it may be the conclusion of a formula or several formulas. Asking *what do the figures represent?* begins with asking, *What is being counted or measured?* Once you have determined what is being counted or measured, your next objective is to determine *if* what is being counted or measured is relevant to, or representative of, the phenomenon you are considering in the context of your advocacy. Only through determining what the figures represent can you begin to assess the potential impact of the statistics being offered and determine the extent to which they help or harm your cause. The most common objection that results from asking this question is that the statistics measure something different than what is under consideration in the public policy debate or they are "not representative."

To highlight the importance of determining what statistics "really" represent, you may note the different value of using alternative measures of "central tendency" (i.e., mean, median, and mode) in public controversies, such as, for example, the state of the U.S. economy. If you wish to gauge the health of the economy based on average household incomes, you have three averages from which to choose. If you want to make our economy appear worse, you might use the median as your measure of central tendency – or the value that falls in the center of the available data. According to the U.S. Census Bureau, the median household income in 2011 was $50,054.[21] If you want to paint a sunnier picture of the economy, you might use the mean instead – the sum of a set of numbers divided by the quantity of numbers added. In this case, the mean household income was $69,667[22] – more than 1/3rd greater than the median! Neither one of these averages is, by its nature, more or less accurate; nevertheless, each may tell a different story.

The third question – *What conclusions do the figures support?* – bears on whether the statistics serve any effective purpose. If you are marshaling statistics to support your claims, you can assess whether they do indeed strengthen your argument, and, if they do not, what statistical data might? If you are evaluating the statistics used by another to support a conclusion with which you disagree, you can determine the extent to which you need to invalidate them through objections – the most common being that the figures do not support the claim. It is unlikely in the realm of public policy advocacy that you will have at your reach statistics that support your precise position. One of the reasons statistics are so well-regarded is that, at their best, they are objective facts that are not intended to support any position. Statistics are commonly used by advocates to piece together a picture of sufficiency or insufficiency, to establish a problem and identify a probable cause.

When statistics are used to prove that a proposal will be effective, it is wise to recall the uncertainty that accompanies predictions and observe the manner in which advocates infer from statistics a conclusion. For example, it is common for many universities to require that freshmen live in the residence halls, but some universities have contemplated a second-year residency requirement for sophomores. Often, statistics are used by proponents of such a proposal to illustrate that students who live in the residence halls a second year are more likely to continue into their junior year and to graduate. Do such figures support the conclusion that retention rates will increase if there is a second-year residency requirement? Opponents argue they do not, because there are so many other factors that could have caused the voluntarily returning students to stay enrolled, such as their household income or the enhanced quality of the particular residence halls the returning students lived in. They also note that such statistics do not factor into the equation the potential decline in enrollment that might occur if freshmen, wishing to avoid a mandatory second-year requirement, choose to enroll in another university.

In the next chapter, we consider the practical and ethical issues raised when you contemplate the audience of your advocacy.

Exercise 7: Evaluating Evidence in a Scenario

Consider a current public policy scenario (e.g., gun control, defense spending, stimulus spending) and identify the status quo and the proposition. From there, consider one instance/example of evidence used by each side that comes from an authority and one instance/example of statistics used by each side (for a total of four pieces of evidence). Apply the critical questions to both sets of evidence and assess its overall quality – strengths and/or weaknesses.

Notes

1. Robert P. Newman and Dale R. Newman, *Evidence* (Boston: Houghton Mifflin Co., 1969), 54.
2. Ibid., 55–56.
3. Ibid., 58.
4. Robert James Branham, *Debate and Critical Analysis: The Harmony of Conflict* (Hillsdale, NJ: Lawrence Erlbaum Associates, 1991), 80.
5. Newman and Newman, 62.
6. Branham, 81.
7. Newman and Newman, 62.
8. Ibid., 60.
9. Ibid., 79.
10. Ibid., 66.
11. Ibid., 68.
12. Ibid., 89–203.
13. Alex Jones, *Losing the News: The Future of the News That Feeds Democracy* (Oxford: Oxford University Press, 2009), 2–3.
14. Ibid., 180.
15. Ibid., 180. For more on the "news habit," see Thomas E. Patterson, *Creative Destruction: An Exploratory Look at News on the Internet*, report from the Joan Shorenstein Center on the Press, Politics and Public Policy, August 2007, http://shorensteincenter.org/wp-content/uploads/2012/03/creative_destruction_2007.pdf. For an interview about the results of his study concerning young Americans and the news habit, see Thomas Patterson on "Young People and News," Harvard Kennedy School, accessed September 1, 2014, http://www.hks.harvard.edu/news-events/publications/insight/democratic/thomas-patterson.
16. Jones, 190.
17. Ibid., 202.
18. Karen Bogenschneider and Thomas J. Corbett, *Evidence-Based Policymaking: Insight from Policy-Minded Researchers and Research-Minded Policymakers* (New York: Routledge, 2010), 44–45.
19. Ibid., 34.
20. Newman and Newman, 206.
21. Carmen DeNavas-Walt, Bernadette D. Proctor, and Jessica C. Smith, *Income, Poverty, and Health Insurance Coverage in the United States: 2012*, U.S. Department of Commerce, Bureau of Census, September 2012, https://www.census.gov/prod/2012pubs/p60-243.pdf, Table A-1, 31.
22. Ibid.

· 8 ·

TARGETING YOUR AUDIENCE

Takeaways

1. How you conceive of your audience has ethical implications for how you advocate. Because public policy advocacy is involved in the shared pursuit of good policy, you engage a target audience by analyzing the issue in relation to a community affected by the issue, equipping that community to consider and scrutinize your advocacy.
2. Often, your target audience must be called into existence through your advocacy. Public policy advocacy generates awareness of an issue and calls for interested parties to consider your advocacy and support action related to the issue.
3. Public policy advocacy involves considering carefully who makes up your target audience. This often means knowing as much as you can about the target audience both demographically and psychographically.

Introduction

A good advocate knows the breadth of available evidence, selects the best material from that evidence, and reasons thoughtfully from it with an audience in mind. The core skill for an effective advocate is the ability to craft arguments that are meaningful to an audience. Consider the following example: imagine you are visiting a college campus to advocate for college student loan reform. Before writing your remarks, you anticipate the types of people who will be in attendance: current college students, college graduates, professors, members of the surrounding community, and perhaps a college administrator. An unprepared advocate enters the event intending to convince the whole room, viewing the audience as either one big mass of people or as little more than a random collection of listeners. A better-trained advocate makes careful distinctions among members of the audience, determining who needs to be convinced, who can be convinced, and who may never be convinced. Because your ultimate goal as an advocate is to gain audience support for your proposal, you will be more effective if you formulate some notion of a "target audience" made up of some combination of the larger group. Learn who they are. Consider their knowledge and attitudes toward your subject. Based on this analysis, you may determine the starting points for your advocacy.

In this chapter, we provide a conceptual framework for understanding the audience in the realm of public advocacy and explore some of the ethical and practical implications associated with targeting an audience. We make a case for viewing the target audience as a community to which you, the advocate, belong. We also recommend *issues analysis* over what is commonly referred to as "audience analysis," which we believe is beyond the limited capacity of most ordinary advocates and raises ethical issues in the realm of policymaking. As we have emphasized throughout this book, public policy advocacy is an exercise in carefully considering policy proposals and all of the claims that support them. The audience's consumption of advocacy should involve, primarily, the consideration of evidence and the strength of reasoning offered in support of your various claims.

We noted in chapter one that good argument is ethical. When you consider your relationship to the audience, ethics comes most clearly into view: your advocacy should encourage and equip audiences to carefully consider yours and others' proposals. In light of this perspective, we develop the second part of the chapter, which considers how to frame your advocacy with maximum respect for the autonomy and agency of your target audience.

Audience in Public Policy Advocacy

That you should tailor messages to audiences is universally understood, but you must not forget argument's essential role in shaping good public policy. How you conduct public policy advocacy can range along a continuum from verbal coercion, on one end, to public argument that seeks the best end point or outcome, respecting the autonomy and agency of the audience, on the other. "[A]nonymous public relations apparatchiks" and "barracuda tacticians of modern politics," as they are described by rhetorical scholar Thomas Farrell in *Norms of Rhetorical Culture*, inhabit the verbal coercion end; on the other end are "reform-minded individuals and groups who still hope for more responsive and participatory civic institutions."[1] Coercive public communicators use knowledge of their audience and communication strategies with the exclusive goal of compliance gaining. In many cases, that's what they're paid to do. The coercive approach exhibits less concern for good policy, can erode a community's democratic framework, and casts the entire advocacy enterprise in shades of cynicism. Advocates should aspire to engage in public policy advocacy in pursuit of the best policy outcomes because, as Thomas Goodnight explains, deliberative argument "is a form of argumentation through which citizens test and create social knowledge in order to uncover, assess, and resolve shared problems."[2] Long term, society suffers if bad policy is adopted, so there is no value in short-circuiting the audience's willingness and ability to scrutinize either your claims or the claims of those who oppose your ideas.

Convincing an audience involves crafting arguments that you have reason to believe will improve conditions for your audience. To understand what constitutes a reasonable argument, we turn to rhetorical scholars Chaim Perelman and Lucy Olbrechts-Tyteca's explanation of the "universal audience."[3] This idea of a universal audience figures strongly in our thinking about public policy advocacy. While such an audience exists only in the mind of the advocate, it plays a central role in assessing what is a permissible and meaningful objective for public policy advocacy. Perelman and Olbrechts-Tyteca describe the universal audience as composed of all reasonable and competent people, including those to which an advocate is directly communicating. The advocate's conception of this universally reasonable audience provides a starting point for distinguishing between good arguments and bad arguments. From that point, we developed critical questions based on the assumption that there are universal expectations among members of a community that share a common rationality. This conception of the audience also focuses attention on the quality of evidence and reasoning. Consideration of the universal audience leads you to determine if your conclusions are supported by valid evidence and are well-reasoned. Emphasis in this book, then, is on first determining defensible positions, selecting compelling evidence, and finding convincing ways to reason. The skilled advocate then builds his or her advocacy for target audiences and particular advocacy settings.

Ethics versus Aesthetics

Contemplating a universal audience when developing advocacy does not ensure that your arguments will emerge as logically sound or persuasive to every adult you engage. A universal audience exists only in your mind. And, as a product of your imagination, it is subject to all of the mind's subjective limitations. Nevertheless, the notion of a universal audience and contingent idea that you can develop strong evidence-based, well-reasoned arguments for a community that shares a common rationality gives you something stable to consider when developing your message. Our interest in the notion of a universal audience is not intended to suggest we believe in anything like a perfect or ideal argument or that one can adapt perfectly to their audience. It is more constructive, we believe, to accept that targeting one group of people may cause you to be less effective with another, but there is something to be said about trying your best to present your ideas to as many people as you can and hope that the quality of your appeals, if constructed with the best of intentions to solve real problems that have real consequences for real people, is a worthy pursuit. So, you might as well do the best you can, both in terms of marshaling the best arguments and ensuring audiences give them fair consideration.

The impulse to engage in good policymaking versus the temptation to develop messages that effectively persuade your target audience is a dilemma often discussed among communication scholars. Thomas Farrell describes the tension as one between ethics and aesthetics.[4] This tension, we believe, places real pressure on public policy advocates, who must make some peace with the reality that what *he or she* believes is the best argument must be reconciled with likely audience perceptions of that argument. Ideally, your pursuit of the best policy will push you to produce the most thorough and fact-based arguments you can develop. On the other hand, you must contend with limitations of your audience related to education and experience, and expectations, values, biases, and norms that may largely be unknown to you. Efforts to analyze your audience and adapt your message to their passions, dispositions, fears, and the like constitute the *aesthetic* element of advocacy. Advocates must strike a balance between pursuing truth through argument – an *ethical* pursuit – and persuading by way of *aesthetic* adaptation.

Convinced you are right, should you stop at nothing to convince an audience? Convinced that current student loan policy is harmful to students, should an advocate visit campuses to communicate economic doomsday scenarios to frighten students into accepting his or her thesis? The public sphere is a testing ground of ideas. Public policy advocacy is a means to arrive at good decisions about what should or should not be done. Careful scrutiny of policy proposals should not be countered with efforts to circumvent reason, frighten, distract, or overwhelm an audience. Using every rhetorical instrument at your disposal may include effective techniques for acquiring audience acquiescence, but we maintain that failing to respect or facilitate the audience's capacity to understand and evaluate evidence and attend to the reasoning infrastructure of your advocacy are destructive to the quality of public deliberative outcomes.

Unity of Advocate and Audience

For both ethical and practical reasons, we recommend thinking of the advocate and the audience as united. The model offered by Claude Shannon and Warren Weaver, often cited in communication literature, visually depicts a traditional relationship between a sender and receiver that contrasts with what we are describing.[5] The model invites the interpretation that the receiver of a message is an object to be understood and efficiently persuaded (or informed). The goal of communication, Shannon and Weaver lead students of communication to believe, is to be effective and efficient in the transmission of messages. This relationship is implicit in situations, for example, when a client hires communication professionals to change a corporation's public image or to drive up a political opponent's "negatives." The traditional relationship is further reinforced by communication professionals who use every tool at their disposal to give their employer what he or she paid for, with little consideration for the consequences such techniques may have on individuals or the communities to which they belong. Once an audience is conceived of as an entity separate from the advocate, as the Shannon and Weaver model suggests, it becomes a passive, moldable collective whose compliance is sought with little regard for whether the policy (or marketing) outcome is good for it.

In contrast, we recommend an understanding of advocate and audience as unified by shared cultural assumptions and experiences. This assumption will match the advocacy situations in which you find yourself with more or less precision. When you and your audience actually do belong to the same community and share similar cultural assumptions you will likely be more persuasive than when you have little in common with your audience. In situations wherein there are considerable cultural differences between you and your audience, the onus is on you to learn more about the audience and determine where commonalities overlap. A conservative Mormon in Utah running for mayor of a small rural town, for instance, may have little difficulty crafting messages that resonate with a town predominantly populated with conservative Mormons. This is because both have similar cultural horizons or limits of what is known, knowable, and important. In other situations, advocates and their audiences may have greater differences. Imagine a city like Chicago. No one mayor, regardless of race, ethnicity, religion, or socio-economic status, is going to share commonalities with every constituent. Nevertheless, inasmuch as most constituents are English-speaking U.S. residents, cultural horizons will overlap to some degree. Generally, most will understand appeals to community responsibility, appreciate responsibility to family, share the value of hard work, aspire to improved material conditions, and be motivated by appeals to patriotism. Individually, residents may be different, but they do share some values and aspirations. And when differences between advocate and audience are significant, it is incumbent upon the advocate to determine where their horizons overlap, as it is at these junctures of common ground that advocates find starting points for arguments.

The unity of advocate and audience has implications for how we understand the role of audience in the development of good public policy. The Shannon and Weaver model encourages advocates to view gaining compliance as the endgame of advocacy, inclining advocates to ignore the objections audiences raise and/or treating such objections as a breakdown in understanding or failure to agree. This undermines the goal of public policy advocacy – the pursuit of good policy. Philosopher James Bohman writes that democracy needs "uptake" or listening by both advocate and audience if its outcomes are to have legitimacy.[6] Similarly political scientist Susan Herbst argues that we need to improve our "hard listening" skills in order to strengthen our democracy.[7] All told, public advocacy's value to democracy is compromised when advocates fail to consider public attitudes and objections as legitimate. People who disagree with you are not just people whose minds have yet to be changed. Because the audience is not merely an object to be changed, you must be careful not to approach advocacy events strictly with the intention to alter audience attitudes. That endeavor may fail, but the far more negative consequence of such an approach may be to succeed in gaining compliance in favor of poorly conceived and unwise policy.

Issues Analysis

An alternative to audience analysis with the endgame of compliance gaining is issues analysis. Discerning how an audience understands an issue being argued is essential for an advocate. Though the advocate and the audience usually share some basic community ties, your own perceptions of an issue will often serve as a distorted metric when determining audience understandings. While your own position and rationale for supporting a policy, for instance, is a valuable place to start, your personal investment in the issue may limit your ability to anticipate how others will receive your proposals. It is for this reason that you should engage in issue analysis, the process of identifying the knowledge and attitudes of your target audience toward the issue you are addressing. Doing so enables you to marshal evidence and develop appeals that are more likely to receive fair consideration by the audience.

We advise advocates to consider three matters as a general framework for issues analysis. First, you need to determine the extent to which your target audience exists or needs to be called into existence. Second, once the target audience is imaginable, you need to determine starting points for the argument. Finally, you need to consider audience divisions in terms of demographics and psychographics – or measures of who audience members are and what they think about matters that bear on the issue.

Calling Your Audience into Existence

There is an important distinction between the aggregate group of people that will encounter your message (the audience) and the group of people for whom your message is primarily tailored (the "target audience"). Complicating matters further, your target audience often does not exist until you call it into existence. Philosopher John Dewey's description of "publics" (similar in many ways to target audiences), in his book, *The Public and Its Problems*, is instructive. He describes publics as diffuse and transitory groups of people that coalesce around problems.[8] Target audiences are often diffuse because they consist of people who share an interest in an issue but who do not know each other well or may have never met each other. Target audiences are transitory because they come and go with issue awareness. Dewey attributes public awareness to journalists, though we feel compelled to recognize the role public advocates can play in this process. Skilled advocates possess the ability to call their audience into existence by increasing knowledge and generating interest in an issue.

Because target audiences are impermanent, your task is activating, building, and maintaining them. A woman in California may have next to nothing in common with a man in southern Georgia, but once a governor in Texas, for instance, threatens to further limit a woman's right to an abortion, a large and active public may emerge to consider this issue. This does not happen on its own, however. The public emerges because journalists disseminate information and because advocates work to raise awareness, shape opinions, and coordinate action. Once the controversy diminishes, however, the public may dissipate. Sometimes publics dissipate without any resolution at all.

Creating your target audience is a skill in and of itself. Imagine that you are one of the first people to argue that bisphenol A (BPA) can be harmful to the human body. BPA is commonly found in plastics and on metals and papers. It has been linked to cancer, diabetes, and a host of other hormonal imbalances in lab animals. You reserve time to speak about this harmful substance at the local library and find yourself dismayed when no one shows up. Why? Because no one knows what BPA is. And if it is so alarming, some might ask, "Why isn't everyone talking about it?" Many are silent about BPA because a public of concerned people has not yet been built. Building a public over time is a very challenging task for advocates. This is one of the reasons the stock issue of a problem exists; your description of the problem functions to convince others that there is a problem worth fixing, that it is significant, and that it is something about which others should be concerned. You generate awareness and concern about an issue, and in so doing, create a community of people connected by that shared concern – a target audience. While it will not always be your task to form a target audience, at times the possible need to do so expands the undertaking of advocacy.

Gauging Different Starting Points

Giving careful consideration to your audience involves determining if it possesses developed attitudes, specifically about the controversy. If so, it is essential to know what those attitudes are. We suggest that advocates consider three general types of audiences: *nascent*, *familiar*, and *established*. What you likely will be capable of convincing each type of audience will vary by type. You should think in terms of the metaphorical "distance" you can cover with each audience in a given instance – the distance between what the audience accepts (what we call "starting points") and the "destination," or what you wish the audience to accept. Starting points depend significantly on the issue and the audience's experience with the issue.

When an audience has little or no familiarity with an issue, it is a *nascent audience*. What this audience is willing to accept may be further from your end point than if an audience has a great deal more familiarity. Picture yourself once more addressing the audience described at the start of this chapter. Because the effects of the student loan industry have drawn so little public discussion, you may be safe in assuming that there are few grounds from which to launch a convincing argument for a specific policy. Will the audience accept that student loans can be harmful? Do audience members perceive these loans as having the capacity at all to negatively affect their quality of life? Do they even know how much debt they have? Are they familiar with key language like "subsidized," "unsubsidized," "default," "forbearance," or "deferment?" Faced with a nascent audience, you may need to be less ambitious when attempting to get it to agree with your conclusion. Instead of attempting to persuade the audience to accept your specific proposal, aiming for a less distant destination may be more achievable. Teaching a nascent audience about the nature of the student loan industry, how it works, or what its material effects are on graduates may be a more meaningful and useful objective. Doing so moves your audience toward your ultimate end point, getting it to accept the existence of a problem caused by student loans. Though scaled back, the task of moving a nascent audience from a position of ignorance and/or indifference to an awareness and acceptance of facts that support your claim is no minor one.

The *familiar audience* possesses knowledge of your subject, though it may have no opinion, or a soft opinion, about your proposal. Using the student loan example once more, the familiar audience may be aware that student loan debts are rising, that the availability is driving up the cost of higher education, and that the burden of paying back the loans is making life miserable for many. Regardless of this knowledge, this audience might reasonably assume student loans would not exist if they could do so much harm; after all, these loans ostensibly exist to help, not hurt. Some may feel hypocritical condemning a program on which they themselves rely. Under these circumstances, it becomes your task to build on the accepted facts that both you and the audience share. You should help this audience find a way to reason from these facts to your conclusion.

Your task changes when the audience has more firmly formed opinions about the subject, when it is an *established audience*. Assume your specific goal is to garner support for the specific policy goal of allowing people to include student loan debt in bankruptcy proceedings. Audiences with established opinions may fall into one of three categories: convinced, opposed, and inclined. There is little need for you to work to convince those already in agreement, unless it is to motivate or equip them to act. There is a difference between agreeing with someone and possessing the motivation to act in concert with them. The world is filled with people who behave in ways they know are self-destructive, and so your task when faced with an audience convinced you are correct is to motivate it to act.

Whether to work to convince those opposed to your position depends on your circumstances and needs. Who – How many people? Which different constituencies? – do you need to convince in order to accomplish your policy goal, and what resources do you need to have? No person or group has unlimited resources, and so decisions about audiences have to be made with resources in mind. The challenge in convincing those who are opposed to your position is that you need to dislodge them from their position, which involves challenging accepted facts and values.

There will also be audiences inclined to agree with you, but they may be unaware of the specifics of your proposal. You might assume the grounds supporting your claim are, for the most part, understood and accepted by your audience. As such, your task is to convincingly reason with the inclined audience, working from shared grounds to the specific solution. The stock issues of solution and advantages exist, in large part, for this purpose. They are the standard means of convincing an audience that a policy is desirable. An agreeable audience may be called into existence once it has accepted the problem's existence and significance. Audience members may be convinced to support your specific policy proposal once you explain the policy goals and merits, reasons to believe the policy is both workable and effective, and the advantages.

The final matter of audience type deals with the salience of the issues pertaining to your proposal. While audiences may agree or disagree with your position for different reasons, it is important to note that they will also differ according to how salient your matters of concern are to them. To illustrate, consider an audience that is convinced you are right. Audiences that agree with you will vary by issue salience. Though a group may believe you are right and that your proposal is strong, it may find little reason to care. For example, some may believe food deserts (neighborhoods where healthy food is not sold) exist and contribute to poor nutrition. However, they may also have done nothing to solve the problem. On this matter, they belong to a familiar audience; they accept many facts that point to the problem's existence and are inclined to support efforts to remedy it. They are committed to no specific solution to the problem but would like it solved. It can be said that this is a matter of low salience to them. They care, but for them, it may be "down-list" of other pressing and prominent problems. Advocating to audiences for whom your issue is of low salience means you will need to find ways to explain not just the existence of facts or how reasonable it is to accept your conclusion; you will also need to explain why it matters enough to warrant immediate concern and action.

Analyzing Audience Understanding

Audience attitudes depend on what its members know about an issue and how salient that issue likely is for them. Considering again the hypothetical student loan address, people who have college loans are likely to find the issue to be salient because of the relevance and immediacy of student loans to their lives. On the other hand, this subject may be much less salient for a group of well-to-do senior citizens. If you have college loans, you may exhibit an inclination to support proposals to change the system, assuming that changes are likely to benefit you somehow. Senior citizens, on the other hand, may be opposed or indifferent to such appeals. Audience variations in terms of issue salience, acceptance of grounds, shared values, or inclination toward change make understanding the nature of the audience an integral part of developing compelling advocacy. This section looks at the analysis of "demographics" (descriptions of audience subdivisions) and "psychographics" (descriptions of audience attitudes).

Demographics are statistical descriptions of an audience's subdivisions. These subdivisions may be important to you because such descriptions help delineate different sectors of a target audience. *Who is convinced? Who is inclined to support? Who is opposed? Demographically, do these groups share characteristics, and do these commonalities shed light on matters of issue awareness, salience, and attitude?* Demographics are particularly valuable when they unexpectedly inform us of communities who do not share the same grounds associated with an issue. For instance, people who have a general understanding of Democrats might assume that all Democrats support teachers unions and public schools. A more nuanced look at party demographics reveals that, contrary to the assumptions of many, the majority of African Americans support vouchers or the transfer of public school money to private schools.[9] Awareness of this demographic fact indicates that Democrats generally, and African Americans, proceed from different grounds when considering this issue. Their starting points are different.

In the above example, the demographic of race appears to be related to the attitude about vouchers; however, race is only sometimes a factor in determining knowledge, attitudes, or perspectives on matters of public policy. Instead, demographics often help explain variations in policy positions. Exposure to this issue-specific information helps you determine who among your target audience fits within the various categories of audience uncovered by your issues analysis. Returning to the matter of school vouchers, a closer look at demographics reveals that vouchers are more likely to be supported by people with a low income, suggesting that audience understanding of the voucher issue is likely less a matter of race than one of socio-economic status and the related issue of private school affordability.

When demographics are researched for advocacy purposes, much more is looked at than age, gender, ethnicity, and other commonly considered group characteristics. For advocacy campaigns, a broader net is cast, often with professionally conducted polls and surveys, in order to find unexpected audience configurations. Polls may consider age, gender, ethnicity, regionality, religion, income, profession, hobbies, marriage status, political affiliation, and education. The point of such information is not necessarily to learn if a respondent is Catholic, for instance. Instead, professionals will statistically analyze these responses to find out which demographic characteristics correlate, thus identifying a unique audience, characterized by various shared demographic qualities, that give advocates an opportunity to understand the perspective they may share and thus determine the starting point for advocacy.

It may be possible for you to conduct a far less complex demographic analysis by acquiring a demographic breakdown of the group to which you plan to speak. If you are the student loan advocate, you may ask your host about the university's demographics. If visiting a town library to give a talk on an issue, you may look up demographic statistics at Census.gov (information about the age distribution, number of school-age children, median income, race and ethnicity, rates of home ownership, among other information that may relate to your issue). Political information in many states is available through a state or county board of elections. Of course, if your advocacy effort is well funded, you may also turn to a private consulting firm that studies demographics.

Psychographics provide descriptions of attitudes and values shared by a demographic group. Psychographics can help you answer the question, "What attitudes do senior citizens have about my proposal?" or "What do gays and lesbians think about my issue?" Psychographic analysis may also help explain *why* groups possess their attitudes. Such research is less likely possible without financial resources, and it almost always requires expertise. Nevertheless, such research permits you to identify groups that support your position and to understand better what that support really means. Such research, for example, may help explain why city dwellers of lower socio-economic status often support Democrats even while agreeing with Republicans about vouchers. Psychographic information may be used to understand why certain attitudes are held, how strongly they are held, and how to best address the population that holds them.

Returning to the example of a hypothetical advocacy situation related to student loan debt, the information you've gathered, combined with the general knowledge of who will be attending, will leave you with questions to answer before you prepare your talk. Some of your audience will be motivated to see you speak out of interest in your topic. Others will reluctantly attend in order, perhaps, to earn extra credit for one of their classes. You might decide that you have two audiences you can target: an inclined audience that is familiar with the issue and inclined to consider solutions for it, and a nascent audience that, despite little or no interest in the issue, has student loans or knows people who do. For the inclined audience, which already accepts that the student debt problem needs solving, your primary task is to convincingly describe your proposal and outline the advantages it produces. The nascent audience, on the other hand, will have a different starting point. You will likely decide that audience members will need to both gain acceptance of facts about the existence and significance of the problem and make a case for the cause of the problem. Once you've determined where to start your message, you are significantly more prepared, aware that there is no critical mass for any specific challenge to the status quo. Thus, you know your task is more about creating a larger audience for your solution than it is motivating those inclined to agree to support your specific solution. In short, your advocacy will have a clear target audience, and by identifying clear starting points, you will avoid over-reaching.

In the next chapter, we conclude the text by considering the implications of the setting for advocates, including guidance on how advocates adapt to the "norms" of an advocacy setting, followed by an analysis of three factors of an advocacy setting that will assist you in determining the norms of a particular advocacy setting.

Exercise 8: Considering Audiences and Message

Demonstrate your understanding of the relationship between advocacy and a target audience by "reverse engineering" a message, or reasoning from the message what audience is likely targeted by the message. Begin by identifying an individual or a group/organization that is advocating for a policy. Second, find speeches, op-eds, position papers, or press releases produced by this individual or organization. Third, use your chosen text to identify who (what demographic groups) you believe the advocate is targeting and the starting point from which you believe the advocate is proceeding. If the advocate targeted an established audience, in what category do you believe the audience belonged (convinced, opposed, inclined)? Explain the reason for each determination you made.

Notes

1. Tom Farrell, *Norms of Rhetorical Culture* (New Haven, CT: Yale University Press, 1995), 9, 2.
2. G. Thomas Goodnight, "The Personal, Technical, and Public Spheres of Argument: A Speculative Inquiry into the Art of Public Deliberation," *Journal of the American Forensic Association*, 15 (1982): 214.

3. Chaim Perelman and Lucie Olbrechts-Tyteca, *The New Rhetoric: A Treatise on Argumentation* (South Bend, IN: University of Notre Dame Press, 1991).

4. Farrell's project explains why this tension exists and offers a resolution to the dilemma in a defense of the potential of public advocacy that transcends the distinction; we merely borrow the labels he uses (ethics vs. aesthetics) to generate some critical consideration of audience within the realm of public policy advocacy.

5. Claude Shannon and Warren Weaver, *The Mathematical Theory of Communication* (Urbana: University of Illinois Press, 1949).

6. James Bohman, *Public Deliberation: Pluralism, Complexity, and Democracy* (Cambridge, MA: MIT Press, 2000).

7. Susan Herbst, *Rude Democracy: Civility and Incivility in American Politics* (Philadelphia: Temple University Press, 2010).

8. John Dewey, *The Public and its Problems* (Athens, OH: Swallow Press, 1954).

9. Michael Leo Owen, "Why Blacks Support Vouchers," *The New York Times*, February 26, 2002, accessed February 27, 2014, http://www.nytimes.com/2002/02/26/opinion/why-blacks-support-vouchers.html.

· 9 ·

ADAPTING TO THE ADVOCACY SETTING

Takeaways

1. Effective advocacy requires you to carefully craft your message with the norms and constraints of the advocacy setting in mind.
2. Because context influences audience reception of your message, you should carefully adapt your message to the nature of the occasion, the circumstances of the advocacy event, and the medium you choose to use when you advocate.
3. Mediated advocacy presents many challenges, including altering dramatically a message otherwise presented verbally or in writing. You should use caution when attempting to mediate your advocacy or enhance your presentation with media instruments.

Introduction

The capacity of audiences to reject arguments that are well supported, such as theories of evolution and global warming, despite mountains of evidence in support of both, makes clear that more is operating in an advocacy setting than the exchange of evidence and reasoning. In addition to careful analysis of your target audience's disposition toward the issue, your advocacy should also accommodate the setting. Rhetorical scholar Thomas B. Farrell refers to a "rhetorical forum," or more broadly, "rhetorical culture," when discussing the context or setting for public policy advocacy. A rhetorical forum is, according to Farrell, "the encounter setting which serves as a gathering place for discourse."[1] The "encounter setting" operates according to rules or "norms" that provide "loose but recognizable admission criteria as to who may speak, what may be spoken about, and how they are to be held accountable for what they say and do."[2] Understanding these norms, it is possible also to understand the phenomenon of advocates violating the rules, which may either lead to a failure to effectively convey a message or produce a cultural shift that alters the rules of the forum.

In this chapter we consider the implications of the setting for advocates, beginning with guidance on how advocates adapt to the "norms" of an advocacy setting, followed by an analysis of three factors of an advocacy setting that will assist you in determining the norms of a particular setting: the occasion, the circumstances, and the medium.

Norms and Constraints of an Advocacy Setting

Within an advocacy setting, there are several elements that constrain an advocate's message — what they can and cannot say in a given situation. The term "exigency," which we discuss in more detail below, is commonly used to describe those matters around which the public has coalesced. This may be the occasion, issue, controversy, or crisis the advocate is addressing. Exigencies can also be created by you through your advocacy, when you appear with a compelling message about injustice, discrimination, wrongful death, government corruption, and a host of other concerns. Each exigency will place unique situational demands on you. Particulars of an advocacy setting cause you to accord certain issues more importance than others, which bear on the language, evidence, and reasoning you use. This affects the "invention" of your advocacy, as different issues have unique histories and degrees of importance among a community's stakeholders. A setting influences audience interpretations and your judgments concerning argument content, as well as style, arrangement, and delivery. And, importantly, the advocacy setting both shapes your messages and is shaped by your messages. That is, when you speak on a matter of social importance, what you say and how you say it can alter the norms of the setting.

As a practical matter, when engaging in public policy advocacy, you make choices that consciously or unconsciously determine whether or not you will abide by the advocacy setting's constraints. You will most likely not disrupt the norms of a setting, knowing that there are consequences of doing so, and you may find yourself engaging in advocacy within multiple settings with vastly different norms. One of the authors of this textbook, John Butler, works professionally with labor leaders within the construction trades in and around the city of Chicago and North Central Illinois. He also serves on a public university's board of trustees. These different roles and responsibilities place him in advocacy settings where expectations differ regarding when he should speak, on what matters he should speak, and how his opinions should be expressed. The directness and confidence with which he is expected to speak in the labor environment, and the permissibility for informal speech acts such as jokes and use of profanity, for example, must yield to a more nuanced political style that is more formal, slower paced, and diplomatic when publically deliberating university matters.

The constraints of an advocacy setting come into focus more clearly when advocates sense they or their message may not be welcomed by segments of an audience to which they are speaking. Often, these moments involve a passionate advocate willing to risk the rejection of the audience because the cause is so important to that individual. Examples of advocates who would likely violate the constraints of an advocacy setting in order to convey their position include survivors whose loved ones were slain in battle, were murdered, or died due to neglect or malpractice; political leaders determined to repeal popular laws they believe are flawed; anti-regulation businesspersons seeking to eliminate what they view to be unnecessary restrictions on their right to pursue profits; and religious leaders going door-to-door proselytizing their faith. When your setting and/or subject is less polarizing, however, your advocacy may still necessitate calibrations. You might go beyond knowing who your audience is and tailor your evidence and reasoning according to basic assumptions about that audience. For you, understanding how best to construct and deliver the message requires attention to the norms of the advocacy setting. Your familiarity with a setting may give you enough understanding of a context to determine what should or should not be said. However, if you are not familiar with the setting, you must study its defining characteristics in order to best tailor arguments to it. It might be useful to

spend some time in the setting listening to people talk, learning what subjects are common and how conflicts of opinion are settled. You might ask
whether anyone else has come to discuss your particular subject or issue and
if there were any moments of frustration among audience members. Does the
physical setting and the majority opinion of people within that setting have
any bearing on the subject matter? Whatever your standard message might
be, it would be wise to consider a careful revision to accommodate the more
nuanced expectations of an audience situated within a particular setting.

We believe an analysis of three factors of an advocacy setting will assist
you in determining the norms of a particular setting or rhetorical culture: the
occasion, the circumstances, and the medium.

The Occasion

The occasion is the event that brings you, the audience, and the message
together. *Defined occasions* are typically specific events, and the norms vary
according to the customs and conventions that govern how participants interact with one another in a defined advocacy setting. The customs and conventions include, but are not limited to, such matters as how advocates dress;
what words are used or avoided; the types of evidence deemed acceptable; the
degree of tolerance for anecdotes, lengthy or short presentations, seriousness,
and appreciation for humor; and likely shared values. An example of a defined occasion is a floor debate in the U.S. Senate. Here, who may speak, how
long they may speak, and what words or allusions may or may not be used are
defined in large part by the setting. In contrast, *impromptu occasions* emerge
with little anticipation. Being included in a hastily scheduled conference call
to discuss a campaign strategy or possible response to a controversy is an impromptu occasion. Indeed, being called on during a class – especially when
you are not prepared – is an impromptu occasion. What is considered appropriate in impromptu occasions varies considerably with the context.

When advocating during a defined occasion, you should be familiar with
the customs and conventions of the institution responsible for the occasion.
Failure to familiarize yourself with such customs and conventions risks offend-
ing and alienating your audience. Imagine attending a rural county fair on
the 4th of July that has an "open mic" with a sign inviting people to, "Tell us
what patriotism means to you!" Your politically liberal friend approaches the
mic and begins explaining the value of radical expression, uses profanity, and
sets fire to a small U.S. flag. It would not take long to learn that your friend

has violated the conventions of the occasion and antagonized the audience. Many well-known celebrities have made headlines violating the norms of a particular setting, such as when Marlon Brando, in 1973, sent American Indian Movement activist Sacheen Littlefeather to read a lengthy speech decrying Hollywood's misrepresentation of Native Americans on the occasion of his winning an Academy Award; or when Sinead O'Connor ended a musical performance on Saturday Night Live in 1992 by tearing up a photo of Pope John Paul II. These moments were clear violations; but there are also moments when norms are challenged with great eloquence. In 1993, for example, then-President Bill Clinton presented a speech at the Vietnam War Memorial to the great frustration of thousands of veterans who believed that his protest against the war and failure to serve in the military during his college years disqualified him from speaking on such an occasion and at such a location. Addressing audience resistance, President Clinton opened his speech by remarking:

> Some have suggested that it is wrong for me to be here with you today because I did not agree a quarter of a century ago with the decision made to send the young men and women to battle in Vietnam. Well, so much the better. Here we are celebrating America today. Just as war is freedom's cost, disagreement is freedom's privilege. And we honor it here today.[3]

Directly challenging those who believed nothing he could say would be appropriate, Clinton said, "I ask you, at this monument, can any American be out of place?"[4]

Defined occasions also give you time to prepare and adapt to the setting. Under these circumstances, you may prepare a manuscript, such as acknowledgments directed to hosts and audience members, include quotable and cited evidence, and fit the presentation to the available time.

Impromptu occasions are less clear; with short notice you need to evaluate the setting's circumstances to the best of your ability. Impromptu situations may also enable you to use your message to shape or define the occasion, influencing, perhaps, the expectations of your audience. To understand the role of the occasion in an argument, consider a hypothetical moment at work during which you and other employees are being treated poorly. Imagine your boss asks you and several others to do extra work for which you know you will not be compensated. To the others gathered and in front of the boss, you choose to argue that the employees are being treated unfairly, and you ask the others to leave with you with the aim of demonstrating your solidarity. How will you argue this? You may choose to implore the others to stand up for themselves on the basis of their human dignity. Such an appeal may frame particularly harsh responses from the boss as extremely rude and disrespectful, working to your advantage. Or, you may degrade the boss, arguing that others should not be subjected to his incompetence and stupidity, in which case the norms of the workplace will likely make the boss appear justified in firing you. Either way, this situation highlights the precarious nature of impromptu occasions and the risks associated with them.

There are some impromptu advocacy settings for which you may prepare. For instance, in nearly any protest situation you attend, you should be able to summarize the purpose of the protest in a sentence. The purpose of a protest by the American Tea Party movement is more than to gather conservatives and libertarians together to vent their frustrations. Protests occur to garner public attention for grievances, and the act of protesting is part of a larger performance aimed at folks at home who will see coverage on televised news, in newspapers, or online. For this reason, those who attend such protests should be prepared, in the event they are asked by a journalist to explain what they are doing, to summarize their grievances and demands in a way that encapsulates the point for practical use by those covering the protest. We discuss more about the characteristics of mediated advocacy settings below.

All occasions differ according to their formality. It was noted earlier that spheres of argument differ considerably according to their formality (private, public, and technical). However, there is enough variety of formality within just the realm of the public sphere alone to make it necessary for you to give such matters careful consideration. The U.S. Congress is a public deliberative forum, but speakers are not allowed to malign one another. On the campaign trail, however, candidates may voice vicious public criticisms of their opponents. Then-President George H. W. Bush referred to his vice presidential opponent Senator Al Gore as "Ozone Man" because of his advocacy for controls of ozone-depleting chemicals. Vice presidential candidate Sarah Palin famously accused Senator Barack Obama of "palling around with terrorists." These are both very powerful individuals who held executive offices at the time; nevertheless, the relative informality of the campaign setting allowed them to resort to name-calling.

These advocacy situations demonstrate the constraints that both defined and impromptu occasions place on advocates, which you can manage through careful analysis and an appreciation for the norms of such occasions.

The Circumstances

You should also consider the particular circumstances that led to, and constitute, an advocacy setting, as these circumstances also place constraints on you. Here, we direct you to consider six dimensions of context that together make up the circumstances you should take into account when crafting your advocacy:

1. Exigency
2. Historical Context
3. Relational Context
4. Cultural Context
5. Emotional Context
6. Physical Context

Exigency

Ordinarily, you engage in advocacy over matters of concern shared by you and your audience. These may or may not be matters about which you are already familiar. The matter of concern is the exigency, a phenomenon that triggers your advocacy. Rhetorical scholar Lloyd Bitzer explains that an exigency is "an imperfection marked by urgency" that places constraints on advocates. The exigency is one aspect of what Bitzer termed the "rhetorical situation" that "calls the discourse into existence."[5] You will often encounter events that demand a public response or explanation. However, Bitzer makes clear that every situation does not bring forth a response; nor does every response mean that the situation warranted a response. Consider these different situations involving the same advocate. Nine days following the terrorist attacks that destroyed buildings at the World Trade Center complex on September 11, 2001, President George W. Bush addressed a joint session of Congress. During that address, he stated what questions were likely on the minds of most U.S. residents and provided answers for each. Bush claimed:

> Americans are asking: How will we fight and win this war? We will direct every resource at our command – every means of diplomacy, every tool of intelligence, every instrument of law enforcement, every financial influence, and every necessary weapon of war – to the disruption and to the defeat of the global terror network.[6]

This speech followed a clear exigency – the 9/11 attacks. The attacks were a unique moment because they demanded a response. Across generally known

U.S. history, there had been no precedent for a non-military attack that killed thousands, perpetrated against a nation whose residents had no reasonable expectation that they were the potential targets of an enemy. The American people needed someone to explain and define what had happened and what it meant for the nation. They needed to be told what would happen next and that leaders of the nation had the situation under control. Bush defined the moment as one warranting a large-scale military response.

An instance *without* a clear exigency involved President Bush's campaign to privatize a portion of Social Security. Soon after his re-election in 2004, Bush began a campaign of appearances and speeches advocating an option that would allow people to invest a portion of their Social Security savings in private investment accounts. The Social Security program was facing difficulty, but Bush's challenge was to generate concerns about Social Security where there was little among the general public. Moreover, those who might be especially concerned about this issue – senior citizens – typically believe the status quo program should remain intact. In the absence of an event – or exigency – that triggered a shared desire to solve Social Security's pending bankruptcy, combined with President Bush's lackluster advocacy, his Social Security proposals were dead on arrival. Following his sixty-day nationwide campaign to promote his reforms in 2005, Congress decided not to vote on the matter.

Historical Context

Understanding the historical context involves assessing what history the public has with the exigency. It may not immediately be clear to all advocates why the history of an issue is important. However, familiarity with this history is often necessary to establish your credibility as an informed advocate. You may need to know what led to the present situation, asking, "What got us here?" Other questions might be: Is there a history of an effort to address the matter? Is the public familiar with this history? Are there opposing versions of this history? Who are the allies of the proposal? Who are its opponents? Along what lines do people disagree? Are the lines of disagreement drawn along ideological divisions grounded in some historical context? Are people's identities tied up in their expressions of support or opposition?

If we contrast appeals supporting space exploration in the early 1960s with those made by President George W. Bush forty years later, we see historical context affecting advocacy outcomes. In 1962, on the campus of Rice University, then-President John F. Kennedy presented his appeal for greater investment in what was termed the "space race." The speech's famous line – "We choose to go to the moon in this decade and do the other things, not because they are easy, but because they are hard" – came during a hopeful time for the nation.[7] The economy had come off of decades of growth following the 1929 stock market crash, the United States was seventeen years past the end of World War II and was firmly established as a super power, and the federal budget was running a surplus. It was in this optimistic and financially prosperous context that the president made his appeal to land people on the moon and return them safely home.

Forty-two years later, then-President George W. Bush delivered a speech to NASA outlining his plans for human exploration of the moon and Mars. It is largely credited as the speech marking the end of the space shuttle program. His call to action – "We have undertaken space travel because the desire to explore and understand is part of our character. And that quest has brought tangible benefits that improve our lives in countless ways"– was uninspiring for more reasons than just the selection of words.[8] In the years leading up to the speech, there had not been much enthusiasm for the U.S. space program. Since 1980, appeals for federal spending reductions, combined with dystopian spending-run-amok rhetoric, had become central features in Washington. Three years earlier, terrorists destroyed the World Trade Center and attacked the Pentagon. In response, the United States committed itself to costly wars in Iraq and Afghanistan, both of which fomented divisive popular rhetoric. Just one year earlier, the space shuttle Columbia deteriorated during reentry, claiming the lives of seven astronauts. Adapting to this historical context could have involved Bush calling on Congress for a budget increase commensurate with the expense of achieving the objective. He could have also tried to reconcile the expense of his vision with his own past speeches, the positions of his political party, and the public's anxiety and skepticism about large federal projects. He failed to do these things, and NASA's ambitious Constellation Program, targeting manned flights to the moon and Mars, ended under President Obama because of lack of progress due, in part, to poor funding.

Relational Context

Relational context pertains to the relationship between an advocate and the target audience. The amount and type of familiarity between you and your target audience can affect how messages are crafted and interpreted.

If you are an advocate with whom the target audience has no familiarity, you will need to introduce yourself in order to create familiarity, identification, and credibility. In these instances, you may appear before the target audience with few, if any, negative perceptions against which you must effectively operate, and you are relatively free to craft your own persona. The absence of a relationship can work to your advantage because it is more difficult to attribute your motives to self-interest or group affiliation. Imagine you enter an ongoing statewide public debate about whether to privatize fire safety service. The debate has been divided along party lines for years. All of the key advocates on both sides of the issue are well known. People are entrenched, and no movement is being made. Along you come, and members of the target audience do not know if or why they should either like or dislike you. This lack of familiarity may grant you an opening, an opportunity to be heard and not resisted. The absence of a relationship, however, can bring with it the difficulty of reaching any kind of audience with your message.

Whether there is or is not a relationship between the advocate and the target audience, the advocate needs to know what and how the target audience thinks about the advocate and the topic. When candidates run for office, sometimes they conduct polling to learn their "positives" and "negatives," or positive and negative feelings and associations that voters attach to them (politicians and their polls do in a more systematic way what all public advocates ought to: assess the relationship between themselves and their target audience). A politician the public associates with responsible spending, family, and social justice will encounter less resistance than one associated with scandal, debt spending, and corporate favors. When positive associations are made in regard to you, you may be able to rely on the credibility that this confers. The target audience's familiarity with your history and expertise on a topic may also strengthen your credibility. However, you may want to downplay or directly address negative associations that the target audience makes, particularly when these associations can undermine your credibility.

Cultural Context

In chapter eight, we explained that the advocate and the target audience are quite often part of the same community. This is important, because all arguments are underpinned by often-unspoken assumptions shared by members of that community. To be effective, you should be aware of the community's cultural underpinnings in order to help decide what to include and exclude from your advocacy and what language, evidence, and reasoning strategies make the most sense. Many of these assumptions may just feel like truths to you because they are reaffirmed and reinforced throughout the culture. For this reason, such cultural values may not come to mind in any explicit sense. Instead, you might just rely on language and lines of argument with which your target audience generally agrees. It takes a sensitive advocate to recognize these cultural dynamics.

Intercultural communication scholars have pointed out numerous assumptions about communication that help distinguish cultures. These assumptions operate in every setting in which you find yourself, though they will vary across circumstances and audiences. To illustrate what we mean, we return to a cultural assumption that we mentioned earlier in this book: a culture's general tendency toward instrumental or expressive communication – communicating to execute tasks or help manage relationships, respectively. U.S. residents are generally oriented toward instrumental communication. Though they are, the advocacy setting itself can incline an audience toward expectations of expressivity, depending on the circumstances. Take, for instance, the National Rifle Association's (NRA) response to the Sandy Hook school shootings in 2012. Events like this one, in our view, require public figures to make sense of the tragedy in an empathetic way. This moment surely necessitated expressive communication or talk oriented toward consoling those affected, making sense of the events, and reaffirming commitments to community. It is because the moment demanded expressive talk that the transparently instrumental talk of the NRA was perceived by some as inappropriate. Seven days following the shooting, executive vice president of the NRA, Wayne LaPierre, gave a lengthy statement blaming video games and films, adding,

> Every school in America needs to immediately identify, dedicate and deploy the resources necessary to put … security forces in place … right now. And the National Rifle Association, as America's preeminent trainer of law enforcement and security personnel for the past 50 years – we have 11,000 police training instructors in the NRA – is ready, willing and uniquely qualified to help.[9]

We maintain that LaPierre's proposal was received negatively by many because it was instrumental, when the context called for expressive communication. Whether you agree or disagree with LaPierre, given the timing of his speech, it was unlikely that his audience would be willing to accept the implicit notion that their children died because they'd failed to defend the school against armed intruders.

Because people possess different cultural assumptions depending on the cultures with which they identify, to be an effective advocate you may determine it useful to consider these matters as you construct the content of your message. The assumptions people from different ethnic, national, regional, group-affiliated, or workplace cultures have about the world or their values will vary depending on the strength or salience of individual identities. But, just as the salience of an identity can vary with the advocacy setting, so too can the setting and identity be influenced by your choice of words, evidence, and appeals. Take, for example, the tendency among U.S. voters to respond to individualistic appeals. While the individualistic idea that what people earn is theirs alone seems natural enough to go unquestioned, collectivistic appeals may still appeal to U.S. audiences. The mere existence of U.S. labor unions is testament to this fact. When AFL-CIO President Richard Trumka published an op-ed piece in *The Wall Street Journal* in 2011, advocating for Wisconsin Governor Scott Walker's recall, he argued, "The real question, the one at the heart of our economic debate, is this: Do we continue down a path that delivers virtually all income growth to the richest 1% of Americans, or do we commit to rebuilding a thriving middle class?"[10] This rhetorical question asserts that pure adherence to the values of individualism harms workers, a skillful argument that acknowledges widespread cultural assumptions while finding effective ways to advocate despite them.

Emotional Context

The emotional context involves shared audience emotions that may influence the expectations and reception of a message. Events surrounding your advocacy generate a feeling shared by members of the target audience. This feeling can be strong enough that the audience will have an unstated desire for you to address it in some way. If ignored, an audience may perceive you as detached, out of touch, or cruel.

We find this phenomenon in operation in two advocacy settings wherein President George W. Bush sought to meet the emotional needs of target audiences. Bush was notably successful following the attacks of September 11, 2001, particularly for what has been termed his "bullhorn speech," a seemingly impromptu speech delivered after he climbed atop the massive rubble remaining after the collapse of the World Trade Center. Flanked by rescue workers, Bush said:

Thank you all. I want you all to know … I want you all to know that America today, America today is on bended knee, in prayer for the people whose lives were lost here, for the workers who work here, for the families who mourn. The nation stands with the good people of New York City and New Jersey and Connecticut as we mourn the loss of thousands of our citizens.[11]

Being present at the place of the attack, his presence among the rescue workers, combined with his words and apparent confidence, the president met an emotional need that responded both to the grief and anger held by his audience. He was less successful responding to Hurricane Katrina after much of the Gulf coast, most notably New Orleans, was significantly damaged. On the day following the hurricane, Bush began a vacation in Crawford, Texas. Amid reports of the devastation, Bush ended his vacation early in order to return to Washington, DC. Once there, he delivered what *The New York Times* described as his "worst speech." It continued:

George W. Bush gave one of the worst speeches of his life yesterday, especially given the level of national distress and the need for words of consolation and wisdom. In what seems to be a ritual in this administration, the president appeared a day later than he was needed. He then read an address of a quality more appropriate for an Arbor Day celebration: a long laundry list of pounds of ice, generators and blankets delivered to the stricken Gulf Coast. He advised the public that anybody who wanted to help should send cash, grinned, and promised that everything would work out in the end.[12]

This speech failed to meet the audience's emotional needs, which contributed to its widespread condemnation. His remarks did not include the emotional content that was necessary, thus compounding the problems stemming from the lateness of his address.

Physical Context

The physical context is the concrete setting in which you speak. A skilled advocate will adapt to or alter the physical circumstances in order to meet the demands of the setting. The size of the physical space, its lighting, temperature, arrangement, attendance, density, and decoration can all help shape what your audience expects or will tolerate from you. The grandeur of some U.S. deliberative spaces, such as the House of Representatives and Senate chambers, are remarkable. The size, arrangement, and decoration seem to impose formality, generating expectations for formal dress, language, and linear argument. Most spaces will not be nearly as formal as these, and you might appear to a target audience to be out of place, communicating in an overly formal way in a relatively less formal physical setting. Consider, for example, town halls, school gyms, or community centers. Nearly any physical space can be a deliberative space. Many consequential speeches have been delivered from "soap boxes" and stumps in public spaces. These spaces hardly generate expectations of formality, as the target audience is often those passing by. In fact, the nature of such public settings necessitates some degree of informality and flamboyancy in order to attract an audience. Such displays would be perceived less positively in more formal settings.

Many physical settings can be altered to complement your goals. You can accomplish this most easily by adorning the space with symbols that impart a desired mood to the event or provide visual affirmation of your credibility to address the subject. A politician may want to speak from a raised dais, flanked by flags or bunting. Advocates may also choose to speak in a "town hall" format, surrounding themselves with an audience, thus physically reducing the barriers between themselves and the audience. While the physical setting will not ensure a desired reaction, careful attention to it can help prevent it from limiting the effectiveness of your message.

The Medium

The medium you use to address your target audience is both an important component of the advocacy setting, and, in some cases, may constitute its most significant characteristic. As such, the medium may require more thought than any other factor that makes up the advocacy setting. "Media" is used to refer to many things. Most communication scholars and professionals think of media as a reference to the mechanisms for delivering messages. Rarely is speech or written material referred to as "media," a term more commonly reserved for discussion about the press and/or popular culture productions. The distinction between spoken/written advocacy and advocacy that relies on technology, in our view, is important to your consideration of norms and how best to adapt your message to the dynamics of *mediated advocacy*. To discuss it further and provide you with useful guidance regarding how best to position your advocacy for consumption through a particular medium, we consider briefly in-person public address and written advocacy, and contrast these forms with mediated advocacy. Examining mediated advocacy in this context provides only a limited consideration of the effects of the mode of communication that enhances a message, particularly when you consider the rapidly changing technology individuals have available to assist their advocacy. Our observations in this regard are not intended to form a complete framework for analyzing the impact of media on advocacy; they are only to get you thinking about media as an element of the advocacy setting and encourage you to consider the implications of the particular medium through which your advocacy reaches its target audience.

Public Address and Written Advocacy

Before the widespread use of the Internet, it was fair to say that most advocacy, across the life of an advocate's career and engagement with issues, would involve person-to-person speech or written formats. Today that may no longer be a fair assumption; nonetheless, a good portion of your advocacy will involve you speaking, in person, to a target audience, or addressing a target audience in the rather traditional written formats of letters, fact sheets, position papers, and so forth (even if these are sent to audiences via email or made available online). If you are using your voice to communicate with a target audience that is physically present, the medium is what we refer to as "public address." You may be standing at a lectern, as would be the case if you were addressing a city council or audience gathered to listen to your message. You may be at a table, seated, with notes available while you speak. You might be approaching a legislator "on the rail" in a state capital or after having "called them off the floor." You may be in an office, seated or standing among several others vying for an opportunity to address a decision maker. Most of you have, at the very least, found yourself in a courtroom to address a citation. While this is a forensic environment, it is perhaps the most common reference point for those considering a formal advocacy setting wherein the medium of public address is the norm. Courtrooms are structured formats with rules for who may speak and what they may speak about. You cannot, for the most part, speak until you've been asked a question from an authority figure, typically the presiding judge, and your response must be limited to the information sought by the questioner. In preparation for such a setting, you have no doubt found yourself nervous, even when the matter that brings you to the court is minor. You may wish you could show the judge photos or video that support your claims about what transpired or use a video-conferencing program so you can provide the testimony of a friend who was with you when you received the citation, but courtroom rules may prohibit you from carrying your phone. You might even wish to not appear and send a letter with your attorney, so that you can be at school or at work. For whatever reason, the medium of public address may not work to your full advantage, and when combined with the norms of, and generated by, the occasion and the circumstances examined above, your choices may be further limited.

Advocacy through a written medium is perhaps more common than opportunities to address decision makers in person, as various authority figures may wish to consider your concerns in a complete fashion and reserve person-to-person meetings for questions or additional consideration. Written advocacy offers you a significant advantage, provided the receiver of the communication intends to read the material carefully. In public policy advocacy, issues analyses, fact sheets, and position papers are commonly distributed to decision makers, and much of this content is read only by those closest to the proposals, such as sponsors and co-sponsors of legislation, lobbyists representing the opposition, and so forth. Nevertheless, written advocacy is critical to proper messaging, whereby you seek to coordinate the advocacy of many people working toward the same outcome. Getting your arguments on paper is a somewhat risky activity given that those opposed to your policy proposal may receive the advocacy materials and respond point-by-point in written or spoken advocacy directed to decision makers. Your positions may also change as you interact with decision makers and other stakeholders, and you may find yourself explaining contradictory or inaccurate claims that you put in writing in an early stage of your advocacy. For these reasons, you might choose to reserve written advocacy for proposals and related claims that you have thoroughly reviewed and assembled in as complete a fashion as possible.

For advocates who are foreign-born and/or for whom English is a second language (ESL), their encounter with a public address advocacy setting might be daunting, as translation often becomes necessary, and/or the unique characteristics of the speakers' voice, language choices, nuances of meaning, and other stylistic features are accorded only limited consideration. In rigid public address settings, such as a courtroom, translation challenges can place the ESL speaker/advocate at a serious disadvantage. Add to this environment the anxieties that foreign-born residents may face due to their immigration status, and the public address setting – particularly legal settings or hostile political environments – can be some of the most intimidating settings in which they find themselves. Often ESL advocates will turn to written formats because they can review their written materials with native speakers and reduce translation challenges in their favor.

For different reasons, advocates with communicative disorders or for whom a public address setting is very intimidating may prefer written advocacy as well. To the extent advocates can do so safely, we believe they should push themselves to engage authorities and audiences directly, and not be dissuaded from public address due to disabilities, anxieties, or language barriers. We are optimistic about the potential of public audiences to accommodate an ever-evolving appreciation for alternative personal styles and cultural conventions of communication. One of the authors of this textbook, John Butler, has been challenged throughout his life with a recurring stuttering disability, which manifests as a block that prevents his ability to pronounce certain words in some situations. The disability is set off by unpredictable triggers that cannot be precisely identified, and can come into existence and diminish significantly for extended periods of time. Over many years of practice, in such situations he has learned to instantly replace words he cannot say with alternative words he can say – which, to most listeners, results in a hardly noticeable delay or slightly awkward phrase. His ability to adapt to and today regularly participate in public advocacy situations is a direct result of continuing to expose himself to advocacy situations despite the disability (indeed, he has made it his expertise).[13]

For the most part, the lessons in this textbook are offered with public address and written media in mind. It is a common characteristic of textbooks concerning communication skills and performance to offer guidance as if the readers' encounters will be in person or in writing in what might be called "traditional" advocacy settings. This, of course, is not realistic in this age of email, smartphones, Facebook, Twitter, and so forth. For younger generations, advocacy is more likely to be mediated in some form. However, an important assumption guiding this privileging of spoken/written advocacy is that the mastery of such practical skills will offer you the widest range of adaptation capacity and that physical presence is ultimately necessary in nearly all effective public policy endeavors. That is, while certain characteristics of public address and written advocacy may not be relevant in mediated advocacy – permissibility of expositional speech or text or regulation of volume, rate, tone, pronunciation, and cadence, for example – the fundamentals of advocacy are often best learned when envisioned as a person-to-person, direct exchange.

Mediated Advocacy

While we have written this textbook as a practical guide to advocacy situations in which participants are presumed to be speaking or writing their advocacy, and believe that to be the most useful approach for learning about public policy advocacy, we also believe it is important to spend some time considering mediated advocacy. Mediated advocacy is distinguished from public address and written advocacy, even though we have already explained that spoken and written advocacy are forms of media. We do not wish to make too fine a distinction here; but, we do wish to draw attention to the implications of your use of media that enhance spoken and written messages and how these media alter how your advocacy is understood by a target audience compared to how messages are understood by audiences that are physically present. Mediated messages can still be written and spoken, but they are distinguished by their delivery systems and the potential size of the audience. One way to consider this notion of a delivery system and size of a target audience is to think of the concept of *extension*. Media permits an advocate to extend his or her message beyond those immediately present. Written messages can be directed to a mass audience through print duplication and physical distribution (newspapers, magazines, journals) or distribution through electronic means (the Internet, blogs, email, texts). Spoken messages can appear in video form (broadcast TV, Skype, FaceTime, YouTube) and audio form (telephone, radio, podcasts). In this framework, an advocacy letter you write to a university administrator, for example, is not mediated advocacy; however, if you distribute that letter widely through email or ask that it be published in the campus newspaper, it becomes mediated advocacy.

In this section, we consider some of the conventions of the mass media environment, treating media as an advocacy setting with norms that will affect the quality of your messages. Conventions of mass media are common characteristics of information delivered in mass media outlets, such as newspapers and television. In changing media environments, you should be aware of and accommodate these conventions, engage in efforts to control your messages when using a media channel, and determine when it is appropriate to use media instruments to enhance messages. The media is a very diffuse and fluid environment, and it is not our intention to systematically inventory each media form and the unique challenges these environments pose for advocates. Instead, our intention is to share some of our general observations as a means of encouraging your own consideration of what happens to your advocacy when it becomes mediated. We recommend the following general guidance:

1. Determine what you believe can be accomplished through a particular medium based on how the audience generally uses the medium.

2. Consider how your advocacy will be selected, received, perceived, and retained by mass media audiences.
3. Respect the practical limits of the media through which audiences are encountering your advocacy.
4. Structure your advocacy to accommodate editorial preferences and journalistic news conventions, the most significant being that messages be newsworthy.
5. Strive to consciously control your mediated advocacy, particularly its consistency throughout its mediated appearances.
6. Understand the potential that media instruments have to enhance your messages, but be aware that they should be used cautiously.

First, *you should determine what can be accomplished through a particular medium based on how the audience generally uses the medium.* The most significant adaptation typically concerns the length of the information you are presenting and how the media format requires reduction of your message to less complex and detailed treatments of a subject. Your assumption may be that a good argument is a thorough argument, that the more evidence you can marshal, the more influential you will be. However, when you apply that assumption to the world of print media, for example, you may be in for a rude awakening. The op-ed policy of *The New York Times* recommends 750 words. This is the equivalent of three double-spaced typewritten pages. Letters to the editor at the same publication should be no longer than 150 words – less than a page! The Paul Krugman editorial mentioned in chapter two titled "Fear Strikes Out" was only 826 words – well-adapted to the limits of print media.[14] And, these limits are not arbitrary; they reflect both the practical limits of the medium and the tolerances of the audience.

Second, *you should consider how your advocacy will be selected, received, perceived, and retained by mass media audiences.* As we widen consideration beyond print media, the length of information, while still an important factor, explains only part of what causes audiences to prefer certain media over others. Many of the effects of mass media are consequences of the way audiences use media – how they select what to consider and how they receive, perceive, and retain messages within the mass media. Many politically liberal news consumers choose not to watch Fox News, for example, because they are inclined to disagree with the way the Fox network characterizes the news. Instead, they may watch MSNBC, generally considered a politically liberal source of information. In so doing, it may matter less if MSNBC commentator Rachel

PUBLIC POLICY ARGUMENTATION AND DEBATE

Maddow changed their minds about anything and more about whether Maddow's comments reinforce their attitudes. Maddow's loyal audience may tune in more out of habit than because of a specific information need. Or, it may be that they seek a reward that the particular medium is capable of delivering, such as when, during a presidential election, politically liberal viewers tune into politically liberal media to acquire relief from the fear that a conservative will win the White House. The concept of habit is important to understanding why people rely on certain types of media for information about public issues. You should endeavor to adapt to the realities of audience consumption habits instead of hoping that your message will be compelling enough to overcome the fact that nobody's likely to encounter your message through their selected medium.

Third, *if you wish to compete successfully for the attention of media users, you should respect the practical limits of the media through which audiences are encountering your advocacy.* In the present media environment, advocates are always competing for attention with other media. Smartphones, tablets, and laptops make for rich forms of entertainment available at users' fingertips. Once these means are engaged by you, practical limitations will present themselves. According to the standards for many public print outlets today, Krugman's 826-word column is lengthy. The Notes feature on Facebook, for example, allows members to write lengthy posts; however, almost no one writes or reads lengthy Facebook posts. In fact, given the algorithm Facebook uses, all of your friends will not likely see your post unless other friends begin "liking" or commenting on it. Images and short phrases are intrinsic to Twitter messages, which famously allow only 140 characters per message. Brevity, however, neither limits its power nor its reach. Calling on legislators to vote on background checks for gun purchasers, on April 10, 2013, President Obama's Twitter feed stated, "'We do deserve a vote.' – Jillian Soto, sister of Victoria Soto, a first-grade teacher killed in Newtown."[15] His tweet was nicely tailored to the 140-character limit imposed by Twitter. It also included a link to a picture of the president and Jillian Soto with their arms around each other. Such a tweet can raise awareness, help call people to action, and link readers to more developed and evidence-based treatments on a topic.

Internet news sources and blogs, a distinction that gets blurrier by the day, are outlets for relatively more-developed advocacy. You can be your own editor (producing your own blog, for instance), or you can seek to be featured in someone else's blog or news source. Self-edited blogs have the advantage of allowing you to say and do whatever you wish. Alternatively, seeking to advocate through someone else's news site or blog has the advantage of delivering your message to an already-formed audience, yet it may have the drawback of subjecting your arguments to the editorial choices of the site's editors. According to eBizMBA.com, *The Huffington Post* attracts around 54,000,000 unique monthly visitors,[16] an enormous audience for any advocate, *if* your message survives vetting by its editorial gatekeepers.

Well-funded and attractively produced advocacy on the Internet is often delivered in video. Many people encounter the video "virally" through social media sites like Pinterest, Facebook, and Twitter. People who view the content can share it and may be able to click to a website for more information. Invisible Children's *Kony 2012* and Peter Joseph's *Zeitgeist: The Movie* became viral sensations, exposing their arguments to millions. Producing advocacy of this sort necessitates film and editing tools as well as knowledge about filmic conventions.

Fourth, *you should structure your advocacy to accommodate editorial preferences and journalistic news conventions, the most significant being that messages be newsworthy.* Issues common to many communities often appear on broadcast news, which allows advocates to reach large audiences. However, editorial preferences and journalistic news conventions guide media decision makers, particularly the question of newsworthiness. Newsworthiness is a function of both *interest* and *adaptability* to the news format. Whether what interests you will attract the interests of media decision makers often depends on its value as a spectacle or the size of audience interest. Large public crowds and disruptive protests attract news coverage, because they are provocative events that suggest widespread interest. It is important, however, to note that advocates surrender much control over the narrative journalists apply to protests. Some journalists may feel manipulated into covering manufactured news, and they may avoid covering the event or choose to frame it according to its more negative aspects. The unpredictable and chaotic nature of protests provides ample footage to illustrate both the good and the bad of a large gathering.

You need to consider how you wish to have journalists cover your issue and what to do and not to do in order to obtain favorable coverage. Whether a protest, an interview, or a press conference, you need to consider what headline you wish to have attached to your story. Compare what you want reported with what you believe is the reporter's agenda. The differences between your needs and the journalist's agenda may manifest in the way questions are asked. Are the questions "loaded," or do they make assumptions that you do not accept? You can rephrase the question in your answer to avoid affirming the journalist's assumptions. When communicating with journalists, it is important to know that broadcasters rarely show tolerance for long statements and prefer catchy phrases. Even when U.S. presidents speak, their comments are reduced to just seconds on the evening news, if they are covered at all. Many broadcast news outlets favor short sound bites that are interesting, appealing, and encapsulate the cause behind an event or group's actions. Even when speaking to an immediate audience at an event, intentionally planning to craft and incorporate catchy phrases will help advance your cause by making it appealing for a news outlet.

In addition to using brevity strategically, you must also accommodate the nature of the newsgathering process that may work at cross-purposes with your advocacy. For instance, many media formats do not lend themselves to lengthy spoken stories and other less-disciplined speech acts such as jokes, satire, and the defensive rebuttal of points. You should avoid the temptation to treat an opportunity to speak to a journalist in a conversational style. Even if you know certain journalists well, assume always that they will do their job, even if it means revealing something you asked them not to quote or hoped they would consider irrelevant to the issue being discussed. Stories, in particular, will almost always be edited to fit a very limited time frame, as short as five seconds. You should, therefore, expect to have your words taken out of context, often with the effect of conveying a message you did not intend and one that may be harmful to your cause. If you were, for example, interviewed by a local news channel after having spent hours standing at a rally outdoors, and, in addition to thoughtful statements about the issue that brought you out, you remarked how early you got up that morning or how much your feet hurt, these innocuous statements may be the full extent of the interview that makes it on television. What you cannot know is what others are saying and whether several people complained about their early morning start or sore feet.

Fifth, *you should strive to consciously control your mediated advocacy, particularly its consistency throughout its mediated appearances.* Because different forms of mass media can afford you the ability to broadcast your messages, maintaining rhetorical consistency is essential. This means talking about your cause in consistent ways, both in terms of the reasoning structure and particular language of your advocacy. What mass media gives you in terms of message exposure can be limited by poor message penetration. Many people consume mass media in passive ways. Audiences encounter messages while they are doing something else (driving, cooking, waking up, folding laundry, or consuming other media). To penetrate the attention of an audience, quite often messages must be repeated. As such, when it serves your purpose, the content and rhetorical dynamics of your messages should remain consistent. Repetition is ideal in mediated formats. Politicians often refer to the need to "stay on message" for this very reason. A legislator may devote an entire week or month, for instance, to advocate for a bill. To ensure message exposure, such messages are short, memorable statements designed to capture audience attention.

You should also be aware of the potential for your messages to be "re-purposed" by third parties. Today, it is best to assume that nearly anything you publicly say or do will be recorded and rebroadcast via the Internet. Consequently, you should avoid off-the-cuff remarks on any issue of impor-tance to your advocacy effort. In 2008, then-Senator Barack Obama made a statement to the AARP while running for president, indicating that he would not cut Social Security's cost of living adjustment. Since then, he has proposed doing just that, and numerous online advocates have questioned his consistency, linking clips from his original appeal to the AARP. Talking informally with like-minded thinkers can be as tempting as telling constit-uencies what they want to hear. Once the material is made publicly avail-able, however, it can be edited, re-contextualized, and framed to ridicule or embarrass you.

Finally, *you should understand the potential that media instruments have to enhance your messages, and be aware that they should be used cautiously.* Media instruments you choose to use are tools (Microsoft PowerPoint presenta-tions, charts, audio) that may enhance your advocacy, although use of such instruments alters the quality of messages in ways similar to those described above and thus require similar consideration. Many of the conventions con-cerning audience attention, length of content, the relative value of certain graphics, video footage, and so forth apply to the decision to enhance your advocacy with media instruments. Each of these instruments offers you a means of projecting, extending, and/or repeating your message (either phys-ically repeated or offered to additional audience in video, webcast or webi-nar, or through animated means such as storyboards). Enhancing a message is typically done to increase understanding and make key elements more moving and memorable. Most advocates believe media instruments will en-hance presentations. Because media instruments are capable of changing the fundamental nature of messages, however, we advise using them sparingly or with caution. Visually represented material will be received visually, and its reception may not conform to the logical strategies an advocate seeks to convey. Political scientist Edward Tufte is an award-winning expert in statistical evidence and information design who advises professionals in many fields about the implications of visual displays of information, particularly quantitative information. In his book, *Beautiful Evidence*, Tufte provides readers with effective methods for showing evidence and analytical tools for assessing the credibility of evidence presentations. Tufte explains that serious responsibilities accompany the visual representation of evidence:

> Making an evidence presentation is a moral act as well as an intellectual activity. To maintain standards of quality, relevance, and integrity for evidence, consumers of presentations should insist that presenters be held intellectually and ethically responsible for what they show and tell.[17]

In the realm of public policy advocacy, visual explanations are commonly used to present data an advocate believes supports a particular policy direction. While it would be impossible to summarize all of the ways such visual presentations can mislead, either intentionally or unintentionally, we can encourage careful consideration of the power of images.

Because your daily lives are surrounded by mediated presentations, you may assume that your own presentations may be more credible, professional, and stirring when they too are mediated – or employ media instruments. What this assumption fails to take into consideration is how novel and powerful you can be as an individual public speaker and how much more powerful you can be than an audio clip or a PowerPoint presentation. PowerPoint has existed for over twenty years, and yet the canon of great speeches is still without a single speech that included digitized audiovisual enhancement.

There are times, however, when your advocacy *can* be enhanced with media instruments, when such instruments have tremendous potential to enhance the sensory experience of a spoken presentation, make abstractions more comprehensible, provide recorded evidence, render statistics understandable, or strike a chord with the audience. Consider that visual displays can include video, photographs, color, logos, typography, lighting, space, and data graphics. Audio can add voice and music to a presentation. Cell phone applications and laptops can add instant interactive elements. Unfortunately, many speakers will find themselves less interesting than the media with which they are paired.

Our advice for using media instruments in advocacy presentations is similar to the visual aid advice a student gets in a public speaking course: you should use media instruments only when the instruments help make a point better than you can by vocal delivery alone. Is recorded evidence (videotape, pictures, or audio recordings) necessary to make a point? Can you simply use a quotation or a description? Let's say you have a provocative picture; are you tempted to use the picture because it advances your argument or because it is provocative? For example, if your objective is to explain how the HIV virus is spread as part of an effort to put in place some policy measure to reduce its spread, is it necessary to show an animated image of the virus and to leave it projected on a wall while you speak? If the image neither enhances understanding of your argument nor helps advance your argument, it likely distracts from your efforts to persuade. The same is true for the use of statistics, sound, and imagery for purposes of generating emotional reactions. If you choose to use such instruments, you should do so because their use advances your argument.

Exercise 9: Evaluating Adaptation to Advocacy Settings

Identify an instance of public policy advocacy. This may be a speech, a letter to the editor, or a blog post. Evaluate how well the message you've chosen fits the setting using the principles discussed in this chapter. First, identify the message that you've chosen to analyze. Second, provide an overall evaluation, stating whether you believe the message was or was not well-adapted to the advocacy setting. Third, evaluate the message using the chapter items listed below (explain each of your answers).

A. Was the occasion defined or impromptu?
B. How formal was the occasion?
C. Was there a clear exigency that the message addressed?
D. What is the history between the audience and the issue addressed?
E. What is the relationship between the audience and the advocate?
F. Does culture play an important role in the advocacy setting? In what way? Why do you believe this is so?

G. Does emotion play an important role in the advocacy setting? In what way? Why do you believe this is so?

H. If relevant, does the physical setting play an important role in the advocacy setting? In what way(s)?

I. Identify the medium used for delivery (public address, YouTube video, letter to the editor, blog post, etc.). Considering the advocate's goal, is the message well-adapted to the medium?

Notes

1. Thomas B. Farrell, *Norms of Rhetorical Culture* (New Haven, CT: Yale University Press, 1995), 282.

2. Farrell, 288.

3. Bill Clinton, "Transcript of Clinton Speech at Vietnam War Memorial," *The New York Times*, June 1, 1993, accessed August 22, 2014, http://www.nytimes.com/1993/06/01/us/transcript-of-clinton-speech-at-vietnam-war-memorial.html.

4. Ibid.

5. Lloyd Bitzer, "The Rhetorical Situation," *Philosophy and Rhetoric*, 1 (1968): 1–14.

6. George W. Bush, "Text: President Bush Addresses the Nation," *The Washington Post*, September 20, 2001, accessed August 22, 2014, http://www.washingtonpost.com/wp-srv/nation/specials/attacked/transcripts/bushaddress_092001.html.

7. John F. Kennedy, "John F. Kennedy Moon Speech – Rice University," NASA.gov, September 12, 1962, accessed August 22, 2014, http://er.jsc.nasa.gov/seh/ricetalk.htm.

8. George W. Bush, "President Bush Delivers Remarks on U.S. Space Policy," NASA.gov, January 14, 2004, accessed August 22, 2014, http://www.nasa.gov/pdf/54868main_bush_trans.pdf.

9. "Remarks from the NRA press conference on Sandy Hook school shooting," *The Washington Post*, December 21, 2012, accessed January 20, 2014, http://www.washingtonpost.com/politics/remarks-from-the-nra-press-conference-on-sandy-hook-school-shooting-delivered-on-dec-21-2012-transcript/2012/12/21/bd1841fe-4b88-11e2-a6a6-aabac85e8036_print.html.

10. Richard Trumka, "Scott Walker's False Choice," *The Wall Street Journal*, March 4, 2011, accessed February 13, 2014, http://online.wsj.com/article/SB10001424052748703559604576176601936928690.html.

11. George W. Bush, "Bullhorn Address to Ground Zero Rescue Workers," Americanrhetoric.com, September 14, 2001, accessed August 22, 2014, http://www.americanrhetoric.com/speeches/gwbush911groundzerobullhorn.htm.

12. "Waiting for a Leader," *The New York Times*, September 1, 2005, accessed October 23, 2013, http://www.nytimes.com/2005/09/01/opinion/01thu1.html.

13. We appreciate the fact that not all persons with communicative disabilities can overcome them with practice and determination. We merely wish to encourage all individuals with communicative disabilities to engage in advocacy to the greatest extent possible regardless of the social norms and conventions of public address.

14. Paul Krugman, "Fear Strikes Out," *The New York Times*, March 21, 2010, accessed September 15, 2013, http://www.nytimes.com/2010/03/22/opinion/22krugman.html.
15. Barack Obama, Twitter post, April 20, 2013, https://twitter.com/BarackObama.
16. "Top 15 Most Popular Political Websites," eBizMBA, April 2013, accessed April 17, 2013, http://www.ebizmba.com/articles/political-websites.
17. Edward Tufte, *Beautiful Evidence* (Cheshire, CT: Graphics Press, 2006), 9.

APPENDIX
CRITICAL QUESTIONS

Critical Questions for Evaluating Causal Reasoning:

1. Is the identified cause significant enough to produce the problem?
2. Are there other probable causes that might reasonably produce the problem?
3. Will the proposed solution solve the problem?
4. Is there something about the status quo that will prevent the proposed solution from working?
5. Will the proposed solution cause additional problems or disadvantages not already occurring in the status quo?
6. Is an identified disadvantage the likely result of the proposed solution, or might it be caused by other factors?

Critical Questions for Evaluating Deductive Reasoning; *Categorical Reasoning:*

1. Does the specific case or instance under consideration belong to the general category or rule?
2. Is the specific case or instance under consideration accurate?
3. Are the terms used throughout the argument consistent?

Critical Questions for Evaluating Deductive Reasoning; *Disjunctive Reasoning:*

1. Is the advocate considering all reasonable options?
2. Is the advocate offering good reasons for rejecting options?
3. Are combinations of considered options or other options more reasonable?

Critical Questions for Evaluating Inductive Reasoning:

1. Are the instances cited real occurrences as far as can be determined through reliable evidence?
2. Are the instances representative of the practices, behaviors, activities, or phenomena under consideration?
3. Is a single or limited occurrence compelling enough to indicate a problem?

Critical Questions for Evaluating Reasoning by Analogy; *Literal Analogy:*

1. Are the practices, behaviors, activities, or phenomena being compared similar enough to warrant the policy position being advocated?
2. Can the comparison be characterized as fundamentally flawed or socially offensive?

Critical Questions for Evaluating Reasoning by Analogy; *Figurative Analogy:*

1. Is the comparison offered likely to assist the advocate in his or her effort to gain the support of the audience?
2. Can the comparison be characterized as fundamentally flawed or socially offensive?

Critical Questions for Evaluating Evidence from Authorities:

1. Is the authority known?
2. Does the information offered by the authority support the claim?
3. Is the authority capable of observing the phenomenon the authority claims to understand?
4. Is the information offered by the authority likely to be affected by bias?
5. Is the information offered by the authority accurate?

Newman and Newman's Critical Questions for Evaluating Statistics:[1]

1. Who wants to prove what?
2. What do the figures really represent?
3. What conclusions do the figures support?

Note

1. Robert P. Newman and Dale R. Newman, *Evidence* (Boston: Houghton Mifflin Co., 1969), 206.

BIBLIOGRAPHY

Aristotle. *On Rhetoric: A Theory on Civic Discourse.* Translated by George Kennedy. Oxford: Oxford University Press, 2006.

Bitzer, Lloyd. "The Rhetorical Situation." *Philosophy and Rhetoric,* 1, 1 (January, 1968): 1–14.

Bogenschneider, Karen and Thomas J. Corbett. *Evidence-Based Policymaking: Insight from Policy-Minded Researchers and Research-Minded Policymakers.* New York: Routledge, 2010.

Bohman, James. *Public Deliberation: Pluralism, Complexity, and Democracy.* Cambridge, MA: MIT Press, 2000.

Branham, Robert James. *Debate and Critical Analysis: The Harmony of Conflict.* Hillsdale, NJ: Lawrence Erlbaum Associates, 1991.

Burnham, Gilbert, Shannon Doocy, Elizabeth Dzeng, Riyadh Lafta, and Les Roberts. "The Human Cost of the War in Iraq: A Mortality Study, 2002–2006," *Bloomberg School of Public Health,* December 12, 2012. Accessed September 28, 2013, http://web.mit.edu/CIS/pdf/Human_Cost_of_War.pdf.

Bush, George W. "Bullhorn Address to Ground Zero Rescue Workers." *Americanrhetoric.com,* September 14, 2001. Accessed August 22, 2014, http://www.americanrhetoric.com/speeches/gwbush911groundzerobullhorn.htm.

—. "President Bush Delivers Remarks on U.S. Space Policy." NASA.gov, January 14, 2004. Accessed August 22, 2014, http://www.nasa.gov/pdf/54868main_bush_trans.pdf.

—. "Text: President Bush Addresses the Nation." *The Washington Post,* September 20, 2001. Accessed August 22, 2014. http://www.washingtonpost.com/wp-srv/nation/specials/attacked/transcripts/bushaddress_092001.html.

Byrd, Robert C. *Losing America: Confronting a Reckless and Arrogant Presidency*. New York: W. W. Norton & Company, 2005.

Clinton, Bill. "Transcript of Clinton Speech at Vietnam War Memorial." *The New York Times*, June 1, 1993. Accessed August 22, 2014, http://www.nytimes.com/1993/06/01/us/transcript-of-clinton-speech-at-vietnam-war-memorial.html.

Cooper, Martha. *Analyzing Public Discourse*. Long Grove, IL: Waveland Press, 1989.

DeNavas-Walt Carmen, Bernadette D. Proctor, and Jessica C. Smith. *Income, Poverty, and Health Insurance Coverage in the United States: 2012*, U.S. Department of Commerce, Bureau of Census, September 2012, https://www.census.gov/prod/2012pubs/p60-243.pdf, Table A-1, 31.

Dewey, John. *The Public and its Problems*. Athens, OH: Swallow Press, 1954.

Engel, S. Morris. *With Good Reason: An Introduction to Informal Fallacies*, 2nd ed. New York: St. Martin's Press, 1982.

Farrell, Tom. *Norms of Rhetorical Culture*. New Haven, CT: Yale University Press, 1995.

Goodnight, G. Thomas. "The Personal, Technical, and Public Spheres of Argument: A Speculative Inquiry into the Art of Public Deliberation," *Journal of the American Forensic Association* 15 (Spring, 1982): 214–227.

Herbst, Susan. *Rude Democracy: Civility and Incivility in American Politics*. Philadelphia: Temple University Press, 2010.

Huber, Robert B. *Influencing through Argument*. New York: David McKay Company, 1963.

Huber, Robert B. and Alfred C. Snider. *Influencing through Argument*, updated ed. New York: International Debate Education Association, 2006.

Hultzen, Lee. "Status in Deliberative Analysis." In *The Rhetorical Idiom: Essays in Rhetoric, Oratory, Language, and Drama*, 97–123. Edited by Donald Cross Bryant. Ithaca, NY: Cornell University Press, 1958.

Jewell, Elizabeth J. and Frank Abate. *The New Oxford American Dictionary*, 1st ed., s.v. "grounds." Oxford: Oxford University Press, 2001.

Jones, Alex. *Losing the News: The Future of the News That Feeds Democracy*. Oxford: Oxford University Press, 2009.

Kennedy, John F. "John F. Kennedy Moon Speech – Rice University," NASA.gov, September 12, 1962. Accessed August 22, 2014, http://er.jsc.nasa.gov/seh/ricetalk.htm.

Krugman, Paul. "Fear Strikes Out." *The New York Times*, March 21, 2010. Accessed September 15, 2013, http://www.nytimes.com/2010/03/22/opinion/22krugman.html.

McGee, Michael Calvin. "In Search of the People: A Rhetorical Alternative." *Quarterly Journal of Speech*, 61 (1975): 235–249.

—. "The "Ideograph": A Link between Rhetoric and Ideology." *Quarterly Journal of Speech*, 66 (1980): 1–16.

Mill, John Stewart. *On Liberty*. Boston: Ticknor & Fields, 1863.

Milton, John. *Milton's Areopagatica*. London: Spottiswoode & Co., 1873.

Mitchell, Gordon. "Pedagogical Possibilities for Argumentative Agency in Academic Debate." *Argumentation and Advocacy*, 35, 2 (1998): 41–60.

Monroe, Alan. *Principles of Speech*. Glenview, IL: Scott, Foresman, and Company, 1943.

Newman, Robert R. "Foreign Policy: Decision and Argument." In *Advances in Argumentation Theory and Research*, 318–342. Edited by J. Robert Cox and Charles Arthur Willard. Carbondale: Southern Illinois University Press, 1982.

Newman, Robert R. and Dale R. Newman. *Evidence*. Boston: Houghton Mifflin Company: 1969.

Noelle-Neumann, Elisabeth. *The Spiral of Silence: Public Opinion – Our Social Skin*. Chicago: University of Chicago Press, 1993.

Obama, Barack. Twitter post, April 20, 2013, https://twitter.com/BarackObama.

Olson, Kathryn M. "The Practical Importance of Inherency Analysis for Public Advocates: Rhetorical Leadership in Framing a Supportive Social Climate for Education Reforms," *Journal of Applied Communication Research*, 36, 2 (2008): 219–241.

Olson, Kathryn M. & G. Thomas Goodnight. "Entanglements of Consumption, Cruelty, Privacy, and Fashion: The Social Controversy over Fur." *Quarterly Journal of Speech*, 80, 3 (1994): 249–276.

Owen, Michael Leo. "Why Blacks Support Vouchers." *The New York Times*, February 22, 2002. Accessed February 27, 2014, http://www.nytimes.com/2002/02/26/opinion/why-blacks-support-vouchers.html.

Parsons, Talcott. *The Social System*. Glencoe, IL: Free Press, 1951.

Patterson, Thomas E. "Creative Destruction: An Exploratory Look at News on the Internet," *Joan Shorenstein Center on the Press, Politics and Public Policy*, August 2007. Accessed September 1, 2014, http://shorensteincenter.org/wp-content/uploads/2012/03/creative_destruction_2007.pdf.

Perelman, Chaim and Lucy Olbrechts-Tyteca. *The New Rhetoric: A Treatise on Argumentation*. Translated by John Wilkinson and Purcell Weaver. London: University of Notre Dame Press, 1969.

"A Pre-emptive Strike on Meigs," *Chicago Tribune*, April 1, 2003. Accessed September 1, 2014, http://articles.chicagotribune.com/2003-04-01/news/0304010283_1_meigs-field-mayor-richard-daley-soldier-field.

Reich, Robert. Facebook post, September 5, 2013, https://www.facebook.com/RBReich.

"Remarks from the NRA Press Conference on Sandy Hook School Shooting." *The Washington Post*, December 21, 2012. Accessed January 20, 2014, http://www.washingtonpost.com/politics/remarks-from-the-nra-press-conference-on-sandy-hook-school-shooting-delivered-on-dec-21-2012-transcript/2012/12/21/bd1841fe-4b88-11e2-a6a6-aabac85e8036_print.html.

Shannon, Claude and Warren Weaver. *The Mathematical Theory of Communication*. Urbana: University of Illinois Press, 1948.

Sidgwick, Alfred. *Fallacies: A View of Logic from the Practical Side*. New York: D. Appleton and Company, 1895.

Smith, Catherine F. *Writing Public Policy: A Practical Guide to Communicating in the Policy Making Process*. Oxford: Oxford University Press, 2010.

"Thomas Patterson on Young People and News," *Harvard Kennedy School*, July 12, 2007. Accessed September 1, 2014, http://www.hks.harvard.edu/news-events/publications/insight/democratic/thomas-patterson.

"Top 15 Most Popular Political Websites," *eBizMBA*, April 2013. Accessed April 17, 2013, http://www.ebizmba.com/articles/political-websites.

Toulmin, Stephen. *The Uses of Argument*. Cambridge: Cambridge University Press, 1969.

Trumka, Richard. "Scott Walker's False Choice," *The Wall Street Journal*, March 4, 2011. Accessed February 13, 2014, http://online.wsj.com/article/SB100014240527487035596045 76176601936928690.html.

Tufte, Edward. *Beautiful Evidence*. Cheshire, CT: Graphics Press, 2006.

U.S. Department of Homeland Security. *Exercising Prosecutorial Discretion with Respect to Individuals Who Came to the United States as Children and with Respect to Certain Individuals Who Are the Parents of U.S. Citizens or Permanent Residents*. By Jeh Charles Johnson, Secretary. November 20, 2014. http://www.dhs.gov/sites/default/files/publications/14_1120_memo_deferred_action.pdf.

U.S. Supreme Court. 1919. "U.S. Supreme Court: Abrams vs. U.S., 250 U.S. 616.

"Waiting for a Leader," *The New York Times*, September 1, 2005. Accessed October 23, 2013, http://www.nytimes.com/2005/09/01/opinion/01thu1.html.

Warnick, Barbara and Edward S. Inch. *Critical Thinking and Communication: The Use of Reason in Argument*, 6th ed. Boston: Allyn & Bacon, 2009.

Werman, Marco. *How Iran Might Respond to a U.S. Military Strike on Syria*. PRI Audio, 4:50. September 3, 2013. Accessed September 1, 2014. http://www.theworld.org/2013/09/iran-response-syria-strike/

Weston, Anthony. *A Rulebook for Arguments*. Indianapolis: Hackett Publishing Co., 2009.

Zorn, Eric. "When the Mayor Bulldozed an Airport: Daley's Action Inspired Admiration, Outrage and Amusement," *Chicago Tribune*, April 30, 2011. Accessed September 1, 2014, http://articles.chicagotribune.com/2011-04-30/news/ct-met-zorn-daley-moments-0501-201 10430_1_amusement-outrage-lakefront-airport.

INDEX

C

Causal reasoning *See reasoning*
Cause *See stock issues*
Cicero xii,
Claim *See Toulmin model*
Cooper, Martha v, ix, xii–xiii, 6, 64, 72, 84
Compliance gaining 111, 114–115
Context xvii, 14, Chapter 9
  Cultural xix, 131, 134–136
  Emotional xix, 131, 136–137
  Historical xix, 131–133
  Physical xix, 131, 137–138
  Relational xix, 131, 133–134
Corbet, Thomas J. 104
Costs *See disadvantages*
Counterplan 68
Critical questions xvi, xviii–xix, 43–44,
    47–55, 62–65, 67–68, 71, 73, 75, 80,
    83–84, 89, 93–95, 100–101, 104, 111,
    Appendix
  Authority 95–96
  Causal reasoning 52–56
  Deduction 67–69
  Evidence 80, 83–84, 89, 94
  Figurative analogies 75–76
  Induction 71
  Literal analogies 73
  News media 100–101
  Statistics 104

D

Data *See Toulmin model*
Deductive reasoning *See reasoning*
Deliberative argument 6, 20, 23–24, 51, 111
Demographics 115, 119–121
Dewey, John 116
Disadvantages xv, 2, 50, 52, 55–58, 62–63,
    67–69, 85–86, 88–89, 153
Disjunctive deduction *See reasoning*

E

Enforcement (plank) 33–34, 36–38
Enthymeme 30, 46
Epideictic argument 6
Ethics xvii, xx, 10–11, 109–110, 112–113,
    123
Ethos 83
Evidence xii, xvi–xix, 2, 6–7, 9, 11,
    15, 20, 23, 25, 37, 39, 45,
    57, 59, 64, 69–71, Chapters 6
    and 7, 110, 112–113, 115,
    125–129, 135–136, 143,
    148–149, 154–155
Exigency xix, 126, 131–132
Existential barrier *See inherency analysis*

F

Fallacy xii
  Ad populum 9
  Equivocation 65
  False Analogy 74
Farrell, Thomas B. 111–112, 123, 126
Fiat 37–38
Forensic argument 6, 17, 139
Funding (plank) 33, 35–36, 55

G

Goodnight, Thomas 7, 9, 111

H

Herbst, Susan 114
Holmes, Oliver Wendell 5
Huber, Robert xii–xiii, 14, 48, 59,
    69, 74
Hultzen, Lee 31